TechnoLogic

How to Set Logical Technology Boundaries and Stop the Zombie Apocalypse

TechnoLogic

How to Set Logical Technology Boundaries
and Stop the Zombie Apocalypse

Lee Binz, The HomeScholar

TechnoLogic: How to Set Logical Technology Boundaries and Stop the Zombie Apocalypse
www.TheHomeScholar.com

Copyright © 2016 THE HOMESCHOLAR LLC. All rights reserved. This book may be copied or printed by the original purchaser for personal or family use only. Such reproductions may not be sold or distributed. Except for the above stated authorization to photocopy, no part of this book may be reproduced by any means without written permission of the author.

Disclaimer: Parents assume full responsibility to ensure their children are not affected by the technology-induced zombie apocalypse. We offer no guarantees, written or implied, that the advice contained in this book will ensure children do not stumble into walls, trip over dogs, develop a vitamin D deficiency, or a Facebook psychosis due to an excessive use of their devices. Parents are in the best position to observe and prevent problems, provided, of course, that they occasionally look up from their devices as well.

Printed in the United States of America
Edited by Kimberly Charron

ISBN-13: 9781519100399
ISBN-10: 1519100396

Library of Congress Control Number: 2015919238
CreateSpace Independent Publishing Platform
North Charleston, South Carolina

Table of Contents

Foreword · vii

Acknowledgements · xi

Contributors · xiii

Introduction Technology is a Blessing and a Curse · · · · · · · · · · · · xvii

Understand the Problem · *1*

Chapter 1   Twelve Reasons for Setting Technology Boundaries · · 3

Chapter 2   Why Guidelines are Important · · · · · · · · · · · · · · 39

Face the Problem · *45*

Chapter 3   Eleven Long-term Consequences of Excessive
            Technology Use · 47

Chapter 4   Twelve Symptoms of Serious Technology Abuse · · 65

Chapter 5   The Impact of Technology on
            the Developing Child · 71

Chapter 6   Technology in Education · · · · · · · · · · · · · · · · · 81

Prevent the Problem · *97*

Chapter 7   Ten Ways to Create Wholesome
             Technology Boundaries · 99

Chapter 8   Nine Real Family Examples of Setting
             Successful Technology Boundaries · · · · · · · · · · · 117

Chapter 9   Seven Steps for Safe and Sane Internet Use · · · · 123

Deal With The Problem · *127*

Chapter 10   How to Successfully Unplug: Dealing with
             Troublesome Technology · · · · · · · · · · · · · · · · · · 129

Chapter 11   Helping Children with Digital Addiction · · · · · · 147

Conclusion   Doing Everything Right is No Guarantee · · · · · · 163

About the Author · 169

Resources · *171*

Companion Video Series ·173

Appendix A Critical Technology Boundaries
           for Children and Teens Worksheet · · · · · · · · · · · 175

Appendix B Reference Charts from Zone'in
           Programs Inc. · 179

Appendix C Resources · 183

Appendix D Works Cited · 189

Foreword

Eight per cent of our population, or roughly three million children, have a significant problem with digital media addiction.[1]

A decade ago, we parents were talking about the benefits of family beds and carrying our babies in kangaroo style carriers on our chests. There was a desire to keep them close to enhance our connection and share a deep bond with the hope of guiding them to become trusting, secure adults. Somewhere along the way, culture shifted. We welcomed in the digital age with open arms and became sidetracked with all that came with it: an increase in ADHD and ASD diagnoses, an increase in the number of children taking psychiatric medications, the obesity epidemic, a decline in the percentage of boys graduating college, an increase in mass school shootings, and a tremendous amount of loneliness. Yes, loneliness.

Lee Binz addresses these concerns and so many more as she deftly guides parents through an understanding of the latest information about the dangers that accompany gaming/internet addiction in this valuable book. And Lee doesn't stop there; she also takes on important questions, your questions, and helps parents move forward to face their most challenging parenting issues with renewed confidence. Follow her advice, end the power struggles with your children and teens over their technology use, and be well on your way to rebuilding harmony in your family life.

As a Family Therapist who has been working with children and teens for over 25 years, I often meet with parents who ask me, "How can children and teens complain of being lonely when they are more connected than ever before?" In order to answer this question, we first have to be willing to do two things:

1) Toss out the assumption that online connections are equivalent to real life relationships.
2) Ask the deeper question, "Why did we allow attachment parenting to change and develop into the non-human attachment parenting that has become so prevalent today?"

Of course, digital technology cannot be solely responsible for all of these disturbing cultural trends. But, it is most definitely a factor. Consider that babies and toddlers are learning their ABCs and vocabulary words through apps. Think of the experience of a child sitting on their mom or dad's lap, both looking at a picture book together, the child, hearing his parent's voice read the words out loud and lovingly responding with all of his burbles and squeals. Now envision that same child sitting alone, tapping on the screen of an iPad while a digital voice offers preprogrammed comments. This is what I refer to as non-human attachment parenting. There is no comparison in the quality of these experiences for the child. Children who learn through "shared" activities with their parents have an increased vocabulary, learning more words at an earlier age than do their computer taught peers. We now have the research to back up what seems to be an obvious outcome.

Technology has its strengths and its weaknesses. At its best, it is a tool that parents can use in many beneficial ways. At its worst, it is an addictive crutch that promotes antisocial behavior. Either way, there is no doubt that our culture and the very experience of being human is undergoing a massive change. We also know that digital technology is not going away; in fact, we have every expectation that it will continue to grow in influence as virtual reality ocular eyewear finds its way into our stores.

As parents, the power is ours. We have the power to decide the how, what, and where of the digital technology that we allow into our homes. We have the ability to teach our children how to use technology in a balanced, sustainable manner. Happily, we do not need to do this alone. This marvelous book that you are about to read is full to the brim with information and practical solutions. Even the very best of us can find ourselves lacking in one area or another when it comes to parenting. And this is our opportunity to shine as we dig deeper and challenge ourselves to grow in ways that we never thought existed. So try to shake off the guilt, anger, and regret; give yourselves a hug and remember your tremendous strengths as you practice some new skills with Lee's guidance.

Warmly,
Kim McDaniel, M.A.
Family Therapist, Author, and Parent Coach

Acknowledgements

I would like to express my gratitude to the many people who saw me through the creation of this book - to all those who provided support, talked things over, read, wrote, offered comments, allowed me to quote their remarks, and assisted in the editing, proofreading, and design. Thank you to Todd Wilson, fellow homeschool leader and convention buddy. It was our talks together during conventions that encouraged me to begin this project. Todd was my first interviewee and partner in this project. Thanks to Kim McDaniel, for providing the soft feedback of a professional counselor. Representing the reSTART Center for Digital Sustainability, Kim was the first expert interview I sought. Thank you for gently guiding parents with your wisdom and experience. Thanks to Cris Rowan, who agreed to speak to parents with me on this critical issue. Her support was essential to present the science of this project. A special thanks for allowing me to use her charts and graphs to clarify key points.

Thank you to my husband, Matt, for enabling me to publish this book. He supported and encouraged me the entire time, gently reminding me when months slipped by without working on the book. It was his technical ability that helped me translate interviews and emails into printed word in book form. Thank you to my parents, Betty and Walter, for your ceaseless encouragement and belief in The HomeScholar, and our mission to help other parents. Your inspiration to take my talks and interviews and use them to create projects is the very foundation of this book.

I would also like to thank Kimberly Charron for helping me in the process of organization and editing. Last but not least, thank you to all parents who have shared stories with me. Names were changed when requested, but I know who you are, and I thank you from the bottom of my heart! We needed your stories to encourage other parents to see the light!

Contributors

Todd Wilson

Todd Wilson of Familyman Ministries is the author of *Taming the Techno-Beast, Helping You Understand and Navigate Your Child's Electronic World* book and workbook set.

Todd is a dad, writer, conference speaker, and former pastor. His humor is well known and his down-to-earth "realness" has made him a favorite speaker at homeschool conventions across the country. You may also have heard him speak on Focus on the Family. As founder of Familyman Ministries, his passion and mission are to remind dads and moms of what's most important through weekly emails, seminars, and books.

Todd and his wife, Debbie, homeschool six of their eight children. Two of them have already graduated. They live in Northern Indiana and travel across America in The Familyman Mobile. Learn more at The Familyman website, familymanweb.com. Todd knows what he is talking about and has vast experience talking with parents about technology and many other issues. You can completely trust his knowledge, judgment, and experience as he consults with families around the world.

Todd's Take

Todd's thoughts and comments are found throughout the pages of this book, highlighted in the "Todd's Take" sections. Read his book, Taming the Techno-Beast, Helping You Understand and Navigate Your Child's Electronic World.

Kim McDaniel

Kim McDaniel is the co-author (along with Hilarie Cash) of *Video Games & Your Kids, What Parents Need to Know.*

Kim has provided a lot of guidance and encouragement for this book. A devoted parent, wife, and a professional counselor, she has provided clinical services to families, children, and adolescents for 20 years in a variety of settings, including residential programs, hospitals, and in her own private practice. She's a strong advocate of parents taking control of the role digital media plays in their children's lives. Contact Kim directly at thriveprofessionalcoaching@gmail.com. Kim also recommends the reSTART Center for Digital Sustainability website, netaddictionrecovery.com, for more information and support.

Kim's Corner

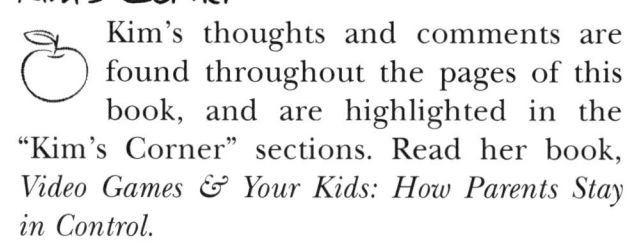

Kim's thoughts and comments are found throughout the pages of this book, and are highlighted in the "Kim's Corner" sections. Read her book, Video Games & Your Kids: How Parents Stay in Control.

Technologic: How to Set Logical Technology Boundaries and Stop the Zombie Apocalypse

Cris Rowan

Cris Rowan is the author of *Virtual Child: The Terrifying Truth About What Technology is Doing to Our Children*. You can find her book, programs, and informational newsletter at Zonein.ca

Cris is a well-known author and speaker to teachers, parents, and therapists throughout North America and in China in the field of sensory integration, learning attention, fine motor skills, and the impact of technology on children's neurological development. Cris has a Bachelor of Science degree in Occupational Therapy and Biology, and is an SIPT-certified pediatric sensory specialist. Cris serves on the committee for the Institute of Digital Media and Child Development, and is the CEO of Zone'in Programs Inc., offering products, workshops, training, and consultations to help promote technology boundaries and enhance productivity. Cris is the creator of the Zone'in, Move'in, Unplug'in, and Live'in educational programs for school and home. Her Foundation Series Workshops help educate parents, teachers, and therapists about how technology affects child development and her Zone'in Training Programs help train other pediatric occupational therapists.

Cris' Counsel
Cris' thoughts and comments are found throughout this book and in the "Cris' Counsel" sections. Read her book, *Virtual Child: The terrifying truth about what technology is doing to children.*

Real Parents and Families Around the World

Real parents have shared their family stories in this book. Some stories are painful but they are always honest and revealing.

Your comments and questions gathered from my work as The HomeScholar have provided much of the inspiration for this book.

Parent's Perspective

Parent feedback and real-life strategies and stories are sprinkled throughout the book in the "Parent's Perspective" sections.

INTRODUCTION

Technology is a Blessing and a Curse

Technology is such a blessing, making our world easier to manage. It can bring people together in wonderful ways, helping humans stay in touch across long distances. I noticed the biggest blessing of all when my children left home and went to college. There's nothing more satisfying than knowing children are alive and well. Seeing their posts on social media is an affirmation our children are thriving. For anxious parents with children far away, it's a relief to know they simply are alive.

Technology is also a curse. It can be used by evil people to cause harm, interrupt normal childhood development, and be overused by innocent people prone to addiction. Thousands of unsuspecting parents and children are at risk in this enticing online world. We have seen people consumed by technology, and perhaps laughingly referred to them as zombies. They walk through the world unaware of their surroundings, noses buried in hand-held devices, or locked in dark rooms staring at computer screens.

Wise parents must educate themselves to be aware of the serious issues regarding technology, so they can steer their children clear of unnecessary bumps in the road on their way to adulthood. We have a responsibility to provide technology boundaries in our own home, on a day-to-day basis.

> *Parent's Perspective*
>
> ♡ "At a weekend party at our house, there was a kid on a video game the entire time. I tried to talk to him and he was like a zombie. I know he isn't autistic, but he was almost mute and bleary eyed."
>
> ~ Anonymous Concerned Mom

I deal with parents from across the globe who have experienced their own zombie apocalypse. I am sharing the stories they have shared with me, with permission. Struggling with technology issues is such a common problem for so many parents that after a while, certain common themes begin to emerge. I've been in the trenches with awesome parents who face unimaginable difficulties. This book draws from my wide-ranging experiences as a registered nurse, consultant, business owner, and friend to many in real life and online.

Yes, there is new technology in the digital age, but some things remain the same. Parents always need to teach their children healthy habits. Setting reasonable digital boundaries creates healthy, happy children. My goal throughout the following pages is to help you create boundaries in your family life (and your own personal life) that will continue to be helpful, regardless of technology changes in the future, solutions that will last.

Will parents listen to the warnings of digital media abuse? When I worked as a nurse, I was often asked, "How do you make people listen when they have a serious medical issue?" It's not always easy. Sometimes you have to be quite blunt and bold. For instance, one of my friends was concerned because her mother needed immediate, serious surgery for a life-threatening condition. Her doctor had told her six months before that surgery was needed, but it was postponed multiple times. The pain became intense. The doctor was rather crass and abrupt on the phone.

Technologic: How to Set Logical Technology Boundaries and Stop the Zombie Apocalypse

He said, "Listen, she will die or be permanently disabled without immediate surgery." My friend was hurt by this doctor's thoughtless, abrupt, and harsh phone call. In my experience, there are two things you can do to make people listen when discussing a serious subject. First, speak gently and explain carefully. Second, if that doesn't motivate people to change their behavior, speak firmly and give shocking and ugly details.

In the pages to follow, I will inform gently and carefully. However, I also need to provide some shock and awe stories, to reveal the ugly details about the dark side of technology. This information is emergency preparedness for prevention, intended to help your child now, and in the event they develop problems in the future. Children can be consumed by so much technology. There are video games, email, text messaging, online chat, instant messaging, photo sharing, social media, blogs, and so much more to engage in. Technology is constantly changing. We need to be prepared to deal with it now and in the future, to prevent serious problems, and take steps towards balance if we notice difficulty.

Unchecked technology exposure can destroy a child's innocence. There is a fixed amount of innocence in a child's life; it is not like a pitcher we can continually fill. The pitcher of innocence is full when a child is born, and gradually empties over time. Our job as parents is to maintain our children's healthy innocence, rather than allow holes in the pitcher too soon. The world will shoot holes through the pitcher in the normal course of living. Without careful attention, the pitcher will be empty before we know it. While we can't avoid all sources of lost innocence, we do have control over the weapon of technology. We need to pay attention to digital media and jealously protect our children's innocence.

Wake up! Pay attention! Misuse of technology is a real and present danger that can hurt our children and us. I encourage you to open your mind to the possibility that the "bright future" of

Lee Binz, The HomeScholar

technological advancement may not be benign. We will look closely together at the hidden dangers lurking in our homes and expose them to the antiseptic of daylight.

Parents must teach children healthy habits, like brushing their teeth and eating their vegetables. Children need to learn healthy habits and why they are important. In the same way, we need to develop healthy habits for using technology. Parents must learn to set technology boundaries for healthy and happy children and teens.

In the upcoming chapters, we will learn to understand the problem of technology abuse, including reasons for setting technology boundaries, and why guidelines are so important. We will face the problem by exploring long-term consequences of excessive technology use, and the symptoms of serious technology abuse. Learn the impact of technology on developing children, and concerns about using technology in education. We will learn to prevent the problem by understanding how to create wholesome boundaries in our homes and exploring real family examples of successful technology boundaries. Learn the steps for safe and sane internet use. Finally, we will learn to deal with the problem with tips on how to unplug and help our teens overcome digital addiction.

This is an eye-opening book that deals with issues only recently recognized by mental health care professionals. It offers hope for parents battling an issue they see but may not truly understand. I hope to equip you to face the sometimes-hard reality of what technology is doing to our culture and our families.

Blessings,
Lee Binz
The HomeScholar

Understand the Problem

CHAPTER 1

Twelve Reasons for Setting Technology Boundaries

It's a new world, with fast-moving changes unimaginable a few years ago. Experts are warning about a problem caused by overuse of technology called "digital dementia."[2] The scope of this problem is huge, insidiously invading unsuspecting minds, like Alzheimer's disease. Children as young as four years old have become so addicted to digital devices that they require psychological treatment.[3] Psychiatrist Dr. Keith Ablow warns that social media "may be considered the tobacco industry of our times - one day facing massive lawsuits for fueling anxiety disorders and mood disorders in millions of people."[4]

In the 1960s, candy cigarettes were available at every corner store, reinforcing the notion to young children that cigarettes were "cool." Tobacco and cigarettes were widely available, including in vending machines. People smoked cigarettes everywhere, with few limitations. Public schools set aside areas for smoking students. Slowly, people learned about the ill effects of cigarettes, and sued the tobacco industry.

Knowing the negatives of technology, individual schools and the education industry continue to emphasize, promote, and encourage excessive online learning. Online classes, programs, and schools have proliferated. Classrooms are filled with computers and hand-held devices for every student, as children are forced to spend more of their day in front of screens.

You might wonder how children can effectively relate to one another and develop real, meaningful friendships and relationships when they are always facing screens instead of people. Children and adults find meaningful friendships by engaging in activities together, not by being glued to a screen. Messaging and texting are not the same as getting to know people in real life, with the nuances of interpersonal communication and non-verbal cues.

Todd's Take

"Technology is changing the face of the world. You can go to any restaurant and see families all over the place where there are two children both on their devices during the course of a meal, with their parents on their phones. I think we're leaving meaningful relationships because meaningful relationships are hard. It's a lot easier to go onto social media and to talk to someone who's always smiling in their picture, and who is always saying happy things. We avoid real relationships in favor of virtual ones."

The recent phenomenon of communicating only on devices has many parents floundering. Thankfully, you can determine boundaries for your own children. There are serious reasons for setting technology boundaries that demonstrate why guidelines are important.

Twelve Reasons for Setting Technology Boundaries

1. Personal Safety

The number one concern about time spent online is personal safety. Teach your children to consider personal safety and not reveal too much online. Children need to understand that everything online is forever - it's permanent, and it can be found. There are so many apps for devices that encourage you to share too much information. An app may promise that a post, photo, video, or text will disappear right after you share it, and be deleted forever, but that's not the case. What is online stays online forever. It leaves a fingerprint that can be traced, sometimes quite easily.

Parent's Perspective

"I have told my kids never to post anything that they wouldn't want to see up on a billboard in the middle of town for everyone to see."

~Nancy

When your child is revealing a lot of personal information online, their personal safety can be at risk. Stalkers and predators are online, looking for vulnerable children, trying to find any piece of information they can. Thieves can also use information shared to find out you're not going to be home and use the opportunity to break in. When you digitally "check in" to a location, everyone can see where you are. Simply revealing where you are can be a threat to personal safety. A criminally minded person can find where you are, or steal your belongings, knowing you are gone.

Criminals keep tabs on social media. The police routinely remind people not to broadcast police activity on social media during police operations because the criminals are watching your posts. They follow posts about police activity, including photos showing where the police are located, to avoid police movement.

It's not only criminals who are tracking you. The Google Maps app tracks your every move on your smartphone, every day, at all times.[5] If you check out the tracking history, you will see every place that Google has followed you using your phone.

What should you avoid sharing on social media? Netsecurity.com lists five posts you should never make on social media.[6] Never share your own or a family member's full birthdate, your relationship status, your current location, the fact that you are home alone, or pictures of your kids that are tagged with their names.

Ill-advised social media posts are regularly visible to the public. Some of my online friends share examples they've witnessed. Lisa mentions seeing a kid posting a photo of their driver's license, which contains so much personal information. Kim notices that many people post about packing for vacation. Melinda thinks it's scary when she sees people post about their activities while on vacation. The worst thing Heather saw was a post by a girl stating she was about to take a nap in her car, giving the exact location on her college campus.

One of my social media friends has a serious medical issue requiring painkillers. She gleefully posted, "I'm going to be taking my narcotics now, so I feel better. I promise I won't wake up for 24 hours." This announcement is like putting a sign on your front door that says, "I've got drugs, and the door's wide open." There are real, potential dangers of sharing too much on social media. These are some of the reasons people choose not to make an account, or restrict their children from creating accounts.

2. Cyber Bullying
Cyber bullying can affect children, whether they are the victims or the bullies. You want to protect your children from cyber bullying and ensure your children don't bully others. Sadly, cyber bullying

Technologic: How to Set Logical Technology Boundaries and Stop the Zombie Apocalypse

is common and peer pressure and teenage confusion mean it isn't only "bad" kids who become bullies, either.

Social media is like a giant public megaphone for bullying. Children seem to think their words don't matter as much when they're online, but the opposite is true. Words posted on social media are broadcast loudly to a wide audience, and the damage can be easily repeated by the simple click of a forward or share button. When words are spoken in person, they are spoken and then gone. When words are shared online, they are forever. New sites and apps are cropping up all the time, and some are perfect for cyber bullying. At least one service allows users to bully other children anonymously and encourages young people to share too much.

Todd's Take

"People are a lot more bold in the things they write when no one can see their face. Sometimes if kids don't know someone in real life, they will say harsher things. If they had known them, it might not be the same."

Even worse, cyber bullying may include sexting. Kids pass around graphic images of others to ridicule them. This behavior, unimagined by your generation, can lead to child pornography charges for the teenagers involved. Even young children and teens have been arrested and charged with child pornography for stupidly taking or forwarding naked pictures of other kids. These inappropriate and explicit photos are often spread throughout groups of children in schools.

In the Chicago area, two suburban middle school students were arrested on child pornography charges.[7] They were accused of texting sexually explicit photos and videos of another student to their classmates. One of the boys sent the original photo and videos to all of his classmates by text message. Another boy in the school also possessed some of this material and disseminated it to his classmates. The boys were 12 years old, and now they each have a child pornography charge on their record.

Stopbullying.gov offers information about bullying and what to do about it.[8] The website explains that cyber bullying is different from schoolyard bullying because it can happen twenty-four hours a day, seven days a week. It can reach your child even when alone, at home. It can happen at any time of the day or night. Cyber bullying messages and images can be posted anonymously and distributed at such lightning speeds that it's difficult, and sometimes even impossible, to track down the source.

The damage done through online bullying and sexting is long lasting. Deleting inappropriate or harassing messages, texts, or pictures is extremely difficult after they have been posted or sent. These online posts have long-lasting effects on the victims. Cyber bully victims are more likely to use alcohol and drugs, skip school, and experience in-person bullying. They may be unwilling to attend school and may perform poorly in their studies, have lower self-esteem, and more health issues.

Parent's Perspective

"Our teen had an old friend open a fake Facebook page, who was framing our son as a racist and sexist who stalked his Facebook friends in order to start a fight at the local mall. They used my son's phone number and eventually posted my son's name as the source behind it."

~Alyssa

Technologic: How to Set Logical Technology Boundaries and Stop the Zombie Apocalypse

---

This is not a problem only in public schools. This is a widespread technology problem. Whether your children go to public school, private school, or homeschool, cyber bullying can still affect your kids.

This generational change in bullying can be shocking to parents. Years ago, bullying was a very personal thing, usually between two people, face-to-face. Between bullying episodes, the child would be safe at home, with parents around to help develop strategies to deal with the individual bully. Now your child can be bullied by hundreds of strangers who don't particularly know or care about them. A child can be victimized by people they have never met, and be bullied based on nothing more than their looks or words alone. It's a struggle to protect your child and defend against cyber bullying.

Todd's Take

"If your children are young, I would not give them a smartphone. This is just Todd not God speaking, but I think sometimes we're giving our kids too much freedom too early. You get a couple of silly kids together, and all of a sudden, you've got something bad because kids do silly things. It's not wise to give young children smart phones, because bad things can happen, and you'll be in a bad place, a place you don't want to be, before you know it."

3. Pornography
According to the American College of Pediatricians, 85% of American teenage boys and 50% of teenage girls have been exposed to pornography. It reviewed the scientific literature on pornography and

published a strong position statement on "The Impact of Pornography on Children."[9] The statement cites the harmful effects of pornography on kids: mental disturbance, mental unrest, anxiety, depression, violent behavior, a young age of first sexual experience, promiscuity, a higher risk of teen pregnancy, and a warped view of male-female relationships. Children who have seen pornography before the age of twelve are more likely to sexually assault other children. Pediatricians are concerned that pornography exposure creates a false idea of human sexuality, which can interfere with the child's future ability to sustain intimate, authentic, stable relationships and marriages.

Parent's Perspective

"Unfortunately, my daughter at twelve saw porn on YouTube at a friend's house and came to ask a lot of questions. I had her mom give me the site to understand what exactly they viewed and it blew my mind. I was heartbroken."

~ ZH

The statement by the American College of Pediatricians also shows that teens and young adults exposed to pornography tend to overestimate the prevalence of sexual activity in society. They are more likely to believe that promiscuity is normal, abstinence is unhealthy, infidelity is acceptable, and marriage is obsolete. Young people exposed to pornography consider rape a less serious crime. Young adult males who have been exposed to pornography are generally more callous towards women and can exhibit sexually aggressive and violent attitudes towards them. They can become addicted to cyber-sex, lose interest in real women, and feel less desire to have children.

Pornography doesn't occur only when adults look for it. Pop-ups and inappropriate images can appear seemingly at random, when

Technologic: How to Set Logical Technology Boundaries and Stop the Zombie Apocalypse

you least expect them. This can happen to your child during innocent internet searches using benign words, and even during school or in online classes. Porn can pop up in an online chat, linked by others and exposed with one innocent click. It can appear on social media profiles, even on sites you might consider safe.

> ### Parent's Perspective
> "My oldest was eleven when first exposed to porn online. We had switched computers and reinstalled software, ending up with a temporary gap in our security software. He was searching for YouTube videos for one of his games, and there it was. I discovered it within a few days, but the exposing damage had already opened a Pandora's Box. It happens SO EASILY now! I wanted to vomit at the time, thinking my little boy had seen some of this stuff. In our case, porn 'kicked' the door open to 'the talk.' My husband and I decided at the time to take the bull by the horns and tackle it all explicitly and directly. As disturbing as the catalyst for this was, it definitely became a blessing we were able to extract from the situation. Our conversations with our eleven-year-old son at that time were some of the most open and bonding times we have had."
> ~ Anonymous Mother

In previous generations, pornography was a local phenomenon. Perhaps a child at school kept a dirty magazine in his desk or at home, sharing it with a small group of friends. Pornographic videos were available to the few people who would venture into an adult bookstore or video store. Transportation, distance, and potentially shame, were involved in accessing pornography. These unnecessary stores have mostly disappeared from neighborhoods. Now the problem is widely dispersed.

With current internet access, it's as if every single family has an adult bookstore or video store in their computer or digital devices, available twenty-four hours a day, seven days a week. These new sources are completely discreet, even while parents are home. Ready at the touch of a button, images can be hidden instantaneously should anyone walk by. As a parent, you may not even know whether your children are using devices and discovering porn while you're in the room with them or asleep at night. It's enough to give parents insomnia!

> *Parent's Perspective*
> "I am finding as a children's minister that many of our third and fourth grade boys are viewing porn."
> ~ Pastor Dave

Unexpected, explicit pop-ups are often the first exposure children have to porn and it's one of the major reasons to keep computers in a public location of your home. If your computers are always facing the public area (in the living room or kitchen), it's easier to supervise your children as they surf the internet. If they come across porn through no fault of their own, your kids may be more easily consoled with a simple reinforcement that it was unintentional. They don't need to hide what happened, as you can quickly explain what happened, without shaming.

Porn can appear on anybody's computer at any time. It doesn't only happen to children. One mom, Kimberly, explains that some of the worst porn she's ever seen popped up on her social media feed as well as during an innocent social media search for a famous composer. Another mother, Debbie, says her boys saw pop-up pornography on her home computer in the living room when they

Technologic: How to Set Logical Technology Boundaries and Stop the Zombie Apocalypse

were about 13 years old. It was so upsetting to the whole family that they were all screaming and didn't know how to turn it off fast enough; they were so desperate to turn off the images. It's terrifying for parents to see these images in front of their children. Desperate to turn it off, nobody wants to stare at the screen to find the little "close" icon.

> ### Parent's Perspective
> "Pop-up pornography happened to me when I was looking for cloth diapers and a whole bunch of pictures of adults in diapers showed up. This was during one of my first searches, years ago, and I didn't realize the stuff that could be called up just using what I thought were innocent words."
>
> ~Nina

The problem is particularly confusing for children who misspell a word, mistake one word for another, or do not recognize the significance or innuendo of an innocent word. Simple typos in an online search can yield pornographic results, discovered innocently. While you might be able to dismiss the results, or recognize the content before opening links, your innocent child or trusting teen may not be as wise.

A LifeSiteNews article explains how quickly it can happen, along with the devastating consequences. The article, "The day my kid found hardcore porn on his iPhone"[10] tells the story of a fourth grade boy who liked to play Minecraft. A typical boy, he thought it would be funny to search for Minecraft underwear mode, so his Minecraft character could play in his underwear. Something else resulted from the search, which progressed to worse search terms. His mother would routinely check his search history, and found out that her fourth grader had begun searching for terms such as "naked people" and then "naked boys" and soon "naked men." The next search his mom found on the phone was, "What is gay?" Further search terms ultimately led him to a pornography video. The mother was shattered and so was her ten-year-old son. She says, "Unfortunately it took him to places he never wanted to go, and he was left wondering about his own sexuality just because he had stumbled upon some naked pictures on the internet."

Parent's Perspective

♡ Suzanne read the article about the ten-year-old boy and it prompted her to look at her eleven-year-old's tablet. She says, "I read in horror the search history. I talked to him immediately and he broke down in tears. My son said he was praying he would get caught. He no longer owns the tablet, and we are not allowing internet, and limiting television. Daily we pray for God to take away the things he has seen ... we are all healing from this."

Stumbling onto pornography is not limited to one location or one device. It does not occur only in your own home or on your own digital devices, either. Consider the public library, which provides technology to the public.

Todd Wilson recalls his first exposure to the internet.

> "The very first time I saw the internet, we were in St. Louis at a museum. We were walking around this display called 'The Internet.' I was pushing the stroller around and I saw about eight or nine guys on different computers. The very first computer I walked by had a scantily clothed woman on the screen. I thought, 'Well, that shouldn't be

up there!' I went to the next guy, looked over his shoulder, and saw the same thing. I am not kidding when I say every single person (they were all men), had a bad image on their screen.

We still seem to think that our children will be better than those men, like maybe our kids can use restraint. They can't. I've had parents who said, 'Oh, we taught our kids that they need to turn away from that stuff and we haven't put up any of these filters or blocks.' Then they come back later and say, 'Well, we had a little issue. They can't have their phones anymore. It's just not safe.' To be honest, we should all be prepared because our kids are going to be exposed. Nobody guards their children closer than me and we still have issues. Don't keep it silent. Don't pretend like it didn't happen. Let other people know."

Parent's Perspective

One mom says, "He had no internet access on the computer but somehow, my eleven-year-old found hardcore porn on the Nook that he used for his homeschool lessons. He was so disturbed and so upset, it took a lot of time and prayer and wise counsel to help him work on getting those images to leave him alone. He's 13 years old now and he wants to serve the Lord. And we are asking the Lord to keep him accountable."

Parents expect to have the birds and the bees talk. Now, you also need to have the pornography talk. When do you talk with your children about this? When do you tell your children that such a thing as pornography even exists? A New York Times article tackled this subject.[11] Experts say that inevitably, your child is going to see pornography at some point. When they see porn, it is never convenient. It never comes at the right time. It's always a bad time to talk about it.

Of course, you must shield your children as much as possible from explicit content, but you also have to accept the facts of life these days. A conversation with your kids is necessary. There is no script for this "porn talk" and no predictable moment to start the conversation. Sometimes it's necessary to have this talk at the age of six or seven, even when your child doesn't understand the basic mechanics of what you're explaining, because they are accidentally exposed to it while exploring online. It's unlikely, perhaps almost impossible, for kids to grow up without stumbling upon some sort of pornographic material online. For this reason, many parents discuss these topics in small bits, as families encounter information, rather than in one big talk. It can be less intimidating. But do not wait until after your child's exposure to mind-altering material. Forewarned is forearmed.

Todd's Take

"Sometimes parents are so scared about it that we jump into the 'porn talk' and we begin to explain too much. I can remember with one of my sons, I was trying to explain that we were putting filters on the internet because there are a lot of crummy images. And he said, 'Like what, Dad?' And I replied simply, 'Just bad stuff.' He went, 'What, Dad?' And I said, 'You know, women.' My son continued with, 'Why?' and I said, 'You know, scantily-clothed women. They're immodest.' It went on like this for a while until I finally said 'Just never mind. It's bad. You're going to have to trust me on this one.' Let your young kids know that

Technologic: How to Set Logical Technology Boundaries and Stop the Zombie Apocalypse

> when you hear that word pornography, it's bad stuff. They don't need to know all the details because it does become enticing at the same time. I wish there was some easy answer. I wish I can say, at 14 ½ you say these 12 words, but it's not that simple. You simply have to know your kids. Maybe you can start by saying, 'Last night they were talking about some kids who got into some bad images on the internet. That's why we're so careful about putting all these restrictions on you.'"

Sometimes your kids won't want to know about porn. That's normal. Other children may have basic questions. Kids seem to have an intuitive sense of when they are ready for the information. You need to be able to read your children so you can give them what they need at the right time. This talk is not something you only need to check off your list.

Kim McDaniel, the co-author of *Video Games & Your Kids* and an advocate of parents taking control of technology in their children's lives, does not recommend a separate porn talk. She suggests parents roll it right into facts of life talks.

Kim's Corner

"When you cover 'the talk' add a discussion on pornography. When you have your first serious talk with your child about sexuality and reproduction, it is a golden opportunity to discuss pornography. Introducing the subject earlier makes it easier to revisit it down the road, but probably no later than age 12, so they hear it from you first."

Kim explains:

> "You want to become comfortable discussing these topics as a parent, and it helps when your child is younger so you can practice how you're going to present it when they get older and need more information. If you have a daughter, this is all a good segue into the topic of plastic surgery and breast augmentation. Girls get harassed about their looks. If you have sons, it's also helpful to discuss your perspective on the subject. The subject of plastic surgery is a more comfortable subject than pornography and will probably provide some good back and forth communication so you can open up a dialogue. Once your child is engaged, the rest of the conversation will be easier. It can be your foot in the door. You want your child to be able to ask you questions now and feel comfortable coming to you when something happens in the future."

Parent's Perspective

"Remember that 'the talk' should not be a single discussion. Kids grow, and while they don't need all the answers up front, eventually they will need more information as they get older. Parts of the talk should start as early as eight. I think the talk must start before twelve unless in an incredibly protected environment."

~Matt

This can be an incredibly difficult thing to handle in a family affected by divorce. Divorced parents need to do their best to put aside their differences, create a united front for the benefit of their children, and discuss boundaries. Sandra shares her stepson's struggle with porn.

"Porn addiction starts as early as ten or sometimes younger now that it's so readily available online. It's extremely hardcore now, even at the entry level - it's creepy and horrible. Once a person is addicted, they are addicted for life. They can get hope, help and healing, but they can't ever undo that addiction, much like drugs in the body. It happens so quickly and their lives are changed forever. Even if it's by accident, it can have a devastating effect. Years ago, my young stepson became addicted to porn. He could no longer come to our home since our much younger daughter was put at risk by his behaviors. He knew it was wrong, but when he was with his mom, there were no boundaries in any areas (including porn), so it was a losing battle. He is a young adult now and it's impacted him terribly."

4. Sleep Disorders
Experts have long recommended not placing a television in the bedroom because late night television viewing can disrupt sleep cycles. Televisions are not the only screens with that effect. Digital devices show similar results, interrupting sleep for teens and adults. People use their phones constantly during the day and think nothing about leaving them on when they go to sleep. When the phone vibrates or sounds, they wake up in the middle of the night to respond. One in four teenagers are awakened throughout the night in this way. According to AOL's third annual email addiction survey,[12] almost half of all people check their email in the middle of the night – half the population is experiencing disrupted sleep!

Technology affects sleep because of cognitive overstimulation. The physical act of responding to a video game, text message, or email gives your body a dose of stress hormones that is part of the fight or flight response. Even if you don't move to touch the gadget during the night, it can cause the stress hormone to pump into your system, making it difficult to go back to sleep again.

Cris' Counsel

"75% of our eight to ten-year-olds have sleep deprivation, which affects their ability to perform academically (U.S. study). A lot of children are lonely and they're using tech as an escape."

Technology needs to be turned off at night. A WebMD article, "Power Down for Better Sleep"[13] claims the key to good rest is turning off gadgets and tuning out. It gives a few simple ways to improve your sleep:

- Unwind before bedtime. Kids and adults should be completely technology-free for 15 to 30 minutes before heading to the bedroom to sleep.
- The bedroom should be an electronic-free zone.
- Cap all unused electrical outlets in the bedrooms to discourage plugging in to recharge in the middle of the night.
- Remove the TV from your child's bedroom, because it can affect sleep quality. Give your child a book to read in bed.

These suggestions may be difficult for some parents to comprehend, even if it seems reasonable to you.

Parent's Perspective

"My son saw porn while searching and watching kid movies. He saw titles of other movies and clicked on them. My son kept trying to get me to set up parental controls on the TV and I kept putting it off because I didn't know how to do it. My son has since helped me set up the parental controls for the

> TV and he doesn't know the password. It shows you that our kids do want healthy boundaries and rules. I also had to set the parental control on my YouTube channel."
>
> ~NH

Other experts advise that children and adults should not use technology within 90 minutes of going to bed. Sleep is disrupted by the light emitted by many electronics, including cell phones, computers, tablets, and TVs. This kind of light can give people a jolt of adrenalin, which is very disruptive to sleep.[14] Rather than debate how many minutes children should be technology-free before bed, focus on the agreement between experts. At least 15 minutes without technology is critical, but 30 to 90 minutes without technology is best for a more healthful night of sleep.

Lee's Lessons

"When my oldest son went to college, he decided that he no longer needed to sleep. He thought sleep was completely overrated and decided not to sleep anymore since he preferred to study all the time. He quickly realized that when he didn't sleep, he had fun studying but his grades went down."

Talk to your children, not only about the importance of sleep, but also about how technology can have a negative impact on their sleep patterns and cause further problems.

5. Situational Awareness
"So this guy walks into a bear ..." It sounds like the beginning of a joke (not real life!) but it happened. A black bear was wandering a neighborhood in California, and came face-to-face with a young

man, head down, texting, without paying attention where he was going.[15] And it's not only bears. You can find many hilarious videos of distracted people walking, bumping into objects, falling into water, or tripping on objects. While these may be some of the funniest videos you can find online, the loss of situational awareness does have a serious side.

Todd's Take
"I think you deserve to be eaten if you bump into a bear while on your cell phone."

Situational awareness means paying attention to where you are, what you're doing, and who is around you. It is usually the first thing women learn in a personal safety class; the instructor talks about how you need to be aware of your surroundings and walk with confidence. It is not possible to keep aware when you're texting or distracted. Teach your kids to pay close attention to where they are and what they're doing.

The most common examples in the news involve texting and driving. You've undoubtedly seen news stories about fatal accidents that occur when the driver is distracted by digital media. Recently in Seattle, a 16-year-old girl hit and killed a child while texting and driving. This doesn't happen only to new drivers, either. Even experienced drivers can cause accidents when distracted by their phones.

And it's not only driving that is hazardous. Even taking a "selfie" with a digital device can be potentially dangerous. One of the growing number of cases of "death by selfie" occurred in Portugal, when a couple was taking a selfie at the edge of a cliff. They were backing up to get a better view for their photo, so they could see more of the cliff in the picture. Tragically, their young children watched as they backed right off the cliff and fell to their death.[16]

Have you or your children ever bumped into anything or tripped and fallen due to focusing on your digital device while walking? Imagine how disastrous this could be in a more dangerous situation, when lives are on the line.

Todd's Take

"I was at a pool and saw a lifeguard jump in to save a drowning kid. They pulled the child over to the edge and the mother who greets him is on her phone. She doesn't even look up at the kid. She just grabs his hand and drags him off as he's coughing and choking. Something's got to change or we're all going to end up dead."

6. Technology Rewires the Brain

One of the scariest aspects of overusing technology is how it can rewire the brain. The increasing awareness of the effects of technology is comparable to the 1960s, when people became aware of the effects of cigarettes. This time, instead of causing lung cancer, technology causes problems with thinking, reasoning, and brain function. It can cause memory problems, difficulty thinking clearly, difficulty paying attention, sad and lonely feelings, an increased risk of suicide in teens, and addiction symptoms. People experience symptoms of withdrawal when they unplug from digital media.

Parent's Perspective

Even adults can feel these symptoms. Ginny says, "I have experienced a lot of these things related to rewiring of the brain. I have noticed that I am unable to pay attention and I am nervous and antsy more than I have ever been." Another mom says, "I've also experienced the rewiring of the brain. I was not ADD as a child, but I tend to be now and I've begun having anxiety issues from too much tech."

Here are five effects of technology, according to the article, "This is How The Internet Is Rewiring Your Brain."[17]

1. Technology use can give you or your child an addict's brain. Unplugging for even a day can give users physical and mental withdrawal symptoms.
2. Social media may make you or your child feel more lonely or jealous. Researchers have dubbed this condition "Facebook Depression."
3. Internet use can increase the risk of teen suicide and self-harm.
4. Technology use can cause memory problems.
5. In moderation, technology use can boost brain function in middle-aged and older adults, so it's not all bad news.

Parents experience these effects as well. Kim confesses feelings of jealousy over some social media posts. A father named Paul acknowledges similar feelings, saying that photos posted by others cause feelings of disappointment, because people don't click on or share his favorite photos that he is most proud of.

According to one study, the more people used a certain social media site, the worse they felt. In this study, "Facebook Makes Us Sadder and Less Satisfied"[18] the research shows that Facebook use has decreased the moment-to-moment happiness and overall satisfaction with life that people report. This is significant because Facebook was the most widespread social media platform at the time. People compare themselves to others on Facebook and often don't feel their lives measure up.

Teach your children the truth about social media. People share only the best about themselves or their families, or the worst. Rarely do they share the day-to-day that fills our lives. I was looking at my photo album the other day, and noticed how many pictures included piles of laundry. I wondered, "Why don't I ever share those photos?" Like others online, I tend to share only photos in which everybody is smiling and laughing, never the messes, laundry, or boxes of junk. As Pastor Steven Furtick, author of *Crash the Chatterbox* says, "The reason we struggle with insecurity is because we compare our behind-the-scenes with everyone else's highlight reel."

7. Limits Normal Growth and Development

Excessive digital use interferes with normal childhood development. Children spend less time in the natural world when their life centers on technology. They spend less time with real books and less time socializing with family and friends.

Those of us who grew up before the turn of this new millennium have noticed a shocking difference in the quality of childhood. Before the wave of digital media, it wasn't uncommon for children and teens to get on their bike on a Saturday morning and ride all day long. Children were outside, active, and making their own fun. As a medical professional, I know that playing in the dirt and snuggling with pets is so important for long-term health, improving physical and mental health. Playing in the natural world, apart from technology, develops an appreciation for nature and the miracle of God's creation. It encourages children to grow up wanting to take care of their natural world.

Lee's Lessons

"With our boys, we had an iron-clad strategy for keeping them focused and out of trouble. First, we involved them in one recreational sport or activity all year round.

Every season of the year we were involved in a sport, whether they excelled or not. We kept them physically active and outside as much as possible, to keep at bay the many possible adolescent traumas. Second, they received a lot of physical affection from their father, in the form of rough housing, wrestling, and athletics."

Since the advent of constant digital media, it's common for children to spend all day on the internet instead of engaged in physical play. Kids are on the internet for school academics, and for fun after school. This has been a serious component in the child obesity problem. Separated from nature, they may lose their desire to be outside and explore the joys of nature, and spontaneous physical play.

Thinking skills are affected. Children are also so used to being served up a constant stream of technology instead of generating their own thought life that they simply aren't used to thinking anymore.

Parent's Perspective

♡ "My sister is a university professor and she told me that just about none of her students know how to think critically. I wonder how much of this is due to a techno generation." ~ Camille

Time away from technology develops critical thinking skills. It's important for children to spend time in the real world as much as possible so they can develop a sense of real world consequences.

Todd's Take

💡 "I think parents have to put our children into those situations. If you give them the choice, they will always choose the easy stuff. They will always choose videos. I mean, we use this sometimes as a babysitter in a bad way. When my kids say, 'Hey Dad, can we go out and do something together?' If I say, 'Why don't you go play on your computer?' they will leave immediately. I don't have to worry about them anymore. It sometimes is a pain but it is better to be intentional and say, 'No, not anymore today.' Limits are good because they'll play those games as opposed to talking to each other. But I think it's up to us as parents to set the boundaries."

Few parents choose to remove digital media from the home entirely. There are times when almost every parent will turn to technology to be the babysitter. Your job is to limit this digital media as much as humanly possible so your children can develop normally, with a variety of different experiences.

Children's brains are pliable and developing, and constant exposure to digital technology is wiring their brains in radically different ways today than in previous generations. An article in Psychology Today explains, "How Technology is Changing the Way Children Think and Focus."[19] The author relates that technology trains the brain to pay attention to information in a different way than reading does. The article quotes Nicholas Carr, who compares the difference between reading books and reading digital media.

"Book reading is like scuba diving in which the diver is submerged in a quiet, visually restricted, slow paced setting with few distractions and, as a result, is required to focus narrowly and think deeply on the limited information that is available to them. In contrast, using the internet is like jet skiing, in which the jet skier is skimming along the surface of the water at high speed, exposed to a broad vista, surrounded by many distractions, and only able to focus fleetingly on any one thing."

Consider the adage, "Give a man a fish and you feed him for a day. Teach a man to fish and you feed him for a lifetime." The internet is like feeding mankind immediate thoughts, and people are not learning how to think for a lifetime. Without learning to fish independently, a person will be dependent on the food provided without effort.

8. Violent Video Games are Linked to Aggression

Multiple studies have correlated video games with aggression and violent video games with decreased positive social behavior. You may have control over which video games your children are playing in the living room, but you don't have control over what your children see or play at a friend's house. You should be aware of everything your children view on devices, social media, and video services.

Even normally well-behaved children can be affected by gaming. Amy shares that her boys act out verbally after playing, even if the video game is not violent. Once your children are demonstrating the effects, the damage of excess is clear. You need to do your best to prevent the damage from occurring.

Parent's Perspective
"I am very concerned about the time today's children spend on digital media

and not connecting with 'real' people - especially the violent video games. I think that the kids can lose the fact that it is a game and not real life, that real people will not get up and be around the next day if they are killed. It could be why we are seeing so much more violence from younger and younger kids."

~Marilyn

Video games can glorify violence. Some popular video games revel in violence for the sake of violence itself. Consider Grand Theft Auto, a game "Rated M" for mature players above the age of 18. It has always been designed to let players loot and murder as their online persona, or avatar. Recently some players of the game have written code to modify the violence of the game to add yet another crime: virtual rape.[20] They record their exploits and post the videos online. If this game is something you allow in the controlled environment of home, what happens when your child searches for Grand Theft Auto online? They could stumble upon these videos of excessive violence during an innocent search for game tips. Children playing the game online could be encountering virtual rape on a server that has been modified.

Although this particular game is rated 18 and up, don't rely on video game ratings for accurate information. The gaming industry polices itself. If possible, play a game yourself before allowing your child to play it, to determine if it is appropriate. It's difficult to give a list of video games you have to look out for, because it's a constantly moving target. There's always something new. Myspace used to be the most popular social media site, and Facebook was "in" while this book was in progress. The current fads will change again. You have to be aware of the constantly moving landscape of digital media.

> ### Todd's Take
> "I once heard a parent foolishly say, 'If my kid ever shows signs of violence, I'm going to stop them.' What does that mean, exactly? If your kid kills somebody, you're going to back off the video games? That seems a little too late to me."

Recognizing violent behavior in your own child can be tricky, because each parent has unique boundaries for their child. Mothers may be able to see aggressive behavior in kids better than fathers, especially with boys who are normally very physical. Moms may seem to understand the difference between normal physical behavior and acting out. When you see your child act differently, talk differently, behave aggressively, or talk incessantly about the games all the time, it's time to reel in those video games.

Your child may try anything to extend their time online. When you are setting limits on screen time, don't fall for the age-old trick, "I'm just watching him play." Screen time is the time spent in front of a screen. If your child chooses to use their time watching their brother or sister, it counts as screen time. Don't give them additional time of their own, or they are essentially doubling their screen time. This seems like an obvious scam, but you'd be surprised by how many parents fall for it.

Todd Wilson describes a time he stumbled upon a group of teenage boys at a camp, talking about riding their bikes and doing other physical things. He thought these boys must be daredevils at first, before he realized they were talking about a video game. Today, kids talk about their games in great depth. They talk to friends and other players on online forums. There is seemingly no end to the possibilities for like-minded fans to discuss the intricacies of individual video games.

Technologic: How to Set Logical Technology Boundaries and Stop the Zombie Apocalypse

Isn't it strange that kids today talk about video games as if they are real? This gives you a sense of how engrossing these games can be. You need to be aware of what is going on. If you notice a game is consuming your child's every waking thought, you need to take action. It may not be the same as problems with aggression, but it's still an indication they are too involved. When you limit screen time, you may begin to notice that your kids quit talking about the games exclusively.

9. Less Social Interaction
Media and technology use is correlated with social withdrawal and isolation. On average, the more someone uses the internet, the greater their risk of serious psychological symptoms, especially in young people. Children may become socially withdrawn and unable to relate to others. In young children, these symptoms can mimic Autism Spectrum Disorder.[21] They exhibit less eye contact when they're glued to the screen, becoming socially withdrawn and less able to communicate with each other.

Kim's Corner
"Children who have existing Autism Spectrum Disorders are more prone to having difficulties with technology and need even more boundaries to help them learn how to cope."

Social media use can cause narcissism, extreme selfishness, and grandiose views of self and personal talents, along with cravings for admiration. You may notice your child becomes less socially adept over time as they use technology more and more.

Todd's Take
"Some kids are socially awkward anyway, even without technology. I think

those kids are even in more danger of being sucked in because it's a safe place to go. They can talk. They can type without even talking. They don't need eye contact. I've seen a pattern of really smart, overachieving kids getting sucked into that world, I think because that world feels so safe. They don't have to fail. They don't have to risk anything. They don't have to disappoint anybody, especially for those kids who are awkward. I would give them even less time on the computer just because I think the draw is so huge."

Increased internet and digital media use has been linked to obsessive-compulsive disorder.[22] Again, this is especially true for young people. This behavior is easy to see in public, where large groups of people seem compelled to check their digital devices.

Todd's Take

"That's one big reason why I got rid of my smart phone. We're on the road a lot, and miss a lot of Sundays at our church. It's really interesting a lot of Facebook users are also checking Facebook on their mobile devices during church! I get those Facebook notifications on my phone even during service times. People are worshipping and checking Facebook at the same time."

People can become so obsessive about their digital devices that they experience the vibrations of incoming messages, even when there are none. Called "Phantom Vibration Syndrome," it can lead you to check your phone constantly, even when nobody is calling or texting.

10. Fidgety Inattention Imitating ADHD

It can be difficult to get your child or teenager to sit and do anything at all without them reaching for their electronic device. Technology grabs the attention with flashing lights, loud noises, and movement on the screen. It can be challenging to keep your child's interest or get their attention away from it. Imagine how difficult it must be for teachers experiencing this constant struggle in school. How can a mere mortal, a simply human teacher, grab the attention of a child who is used to a constant stream of technology?

Electronic gadgets get more enticing every day. Movie theaters have to give elaborate public service announcements before each movie, begging the audience to turn off electronic devices. Few distractions are more annoying than the bright lights or ring tone of a digital device in the row in front of you. Inattentiveness occurs everywhere: in churches, events, and gatherings. In restaurants, parents and children don't pay attention to each other or their meals, but watch their beeping, chiming devices. The next time you're in a public place, look around for families who are paying attention to each other instead of spending more time looking at their phones than enjoying time with their families.

Todd's Take

"When your son or your daughter has to repeat your name more than once, it may mean you're being sucked in by technology. We can expect nothing less from ourselves than we do from our children. I was guilty of that. When my wife would run into the store, my kids would say, 'Hey, Dad ... Dad ... Dad' and I'm checking the weather in the North Pole because I need to see that it's still cold. I just remember this one guy who said, 'If your iPhone is causing you to sin, you should pluck it out.'"

Gadgets are turning us into emotional basket cases.[23] A psychologist was working with a couple who were facing the reality of their children being taken away due to lack of care. Both parents were diagnosed with adult ADHD (Attention Deficit Hyperactivity Disorder), a chronic condition including attention difficulty, hyperactivity, and impulse control. The psychologist tried to coach them in parenting skills so they could regain full custody of their children. During counseling the two parents obsessively, constantly checked their phones, even though the results could be catastrophic to the family if they failed to make progress. Their ADHD was made even worse by the phones.

11. Mental Disorders and Stress-related Illnesses
Technology overuse can ultimately cause serious and severe mental health problems. Consider the rise of school shootings by child perpetrators with mental disorders. These disturbed young children often have something in common; the shooters have been deeply involved in video games. Shooters may be withdrawn, socially awkward, isolated, or have OCD symptoms. These are the same symptoms and consequences of excessive technology use.

One author goes as far as to claim that everyone is going to end up with an "iDisorder."[24] Dr. Larry Rosen coined the term in his book, *iDisorder: Understanding Our Obsession With Technology and Overcoming its Hold on Us.* He believes that most people will begin exhibiting typical signs and symptoms of a psychiatric disorder such as OCD, narcissism, addiction, or ADHD, due to overuse of technology. Dr. Rosen says, "Whether our use of technology makes us exhibit these signs or simply exacerbates our natural tendencies is an open question, but the fact is we are all acting as though we are potentially diagnosable." There is a direct correlation between technology consumption and prevalence of symptoms. The more technology is used, the more a person is likely to show symptoms. Different technologies cause different symptoms, but social media is a major cause of problems.

12. Video Games are Designed to be Addictive
A games researcher at Microsoft with a doctorate degree in behavioral and brain sciences commented on how video games are made to hook players.

> "Each contingency is an arrangement of time, activity, and reward, and there are an infinite number of ways these elements can be combined to produce the pattern of activity you want from your players."[25]

Games are not designed just for fun or enjoyment, but for addictiveness. Game designers use the theories of BF Skinner from modern psychology, the "Skinner Box" to encourage game players with a series of rewards. Your brain doesn't realize your reactions are based on virtual play, but instead act as if they're real, and the random rewards inherent in gaming generate more desire to play.

More game use generates more income for the gaming business. Media companies have psychologists on staff to help them add addictive properties to their digital products. Decades ago, the cigarette manufacturers included all sorts of additives in cigarettes, even sugar, to make them more addictive. Today, it's the media companies pulling this trick. Researchers tweak their games to keep you playing and encourage you to spend money on digital goods.

Gaming manufacturers are dedicated to making their products as addictive as humanly possible. It's serious business and it's the source of their business income. The article, "Kids' Video Games: Source of Fun, Pain and Profit,"[26] claims that video game companies talk openly about creating a compulsion loop. They exploit neuroscience to add addictive properties to their games, and work hard to promote their games to increasingly younger children.

> ### Parent's Perspective
> ♡ "I don't allow violent video games, but I did notice that even after playing seemingly harmless video games, my son would be very grumpy. I saw this several times and just put an end to video games. Only on a very rare or special occasion does he get to play them now."
>
> ~ Chasity

Technology addiction is never beneficial. Not long ago, I received an advertising email with the subject line, "Using the addictive power of video games for education." An educational company was gladly embracing the addictiveness of games and exploiting it to sell educational products. Education should be fun, of course, and including games in education may increase the love of learning. Still, I was shocked. As the mother of a son who is a computer scientist, I know there are benefits of computers in education. As an educational business owner, I know that educational product sales are part of a business operation, but I would never promote addiction of any kind. As a registered nurse, I believe this is a public health concern that should not be taken lightly. I wrote to the company:

> "I am appalled that you would promote using the power of addiction to video games to educate children. It's a serious problem for children, just like gambling addiction or porn addiction, and I would never promote addictive behavior of any kind. 'Harnessing the addictive power of video games for learning' is a marketing phrase I find offensive. I'm sure parents opened that email with that

phrase hoping against hope that their child's behavior is not actually harmful. But that doesn't change the fact that many video games are truly addictive. I doubt if your company would want to use a marketing technique about harnessing the addictive power of alcohol, pot, porn or gambling. Why is the addictive power of video games different?"

The CEO of the company replied and apologized for their poor marketing strategy. The apology fell flat though, when I read their business slogan. My business mission statement is "helping parents homeschool high school." The mission statement of this company is "to use the addictive power of video games for education."[27] Ironically, the CEO of the company is a doctoral student in psychology. Her intentions may be noble, using her training to try to harness addictive power for good, but the bottom line is that addiction is addiction, and something you should avoid and not "harness for good."

You need to be careful about the choices you make. Think about whether encouraging addiction to technology in the name of education might harm your children.

Todd's Take

"I don't like to use gaming and those kinds of things as rewards. I'd rather it just be part of my schedule for my kids. I will never say, 'If you do all this stuff really fast then I will give you game time or I will give you computer time.' I don't want that to be the carrot they're always looking for."

Perhaps you're considering removing all technology from your home: switching off your computers, logging off social media, and ditching the digital devices. Finding a solution isn't that easy, though, because technology is part of your daily life. You may do without one device or application, but your life requires some technology. Your challenge is to find balance and moderation.

Todd's Take

"Keep talking to your kids. I've had parents who say, 'Maybe it will be easier if we just got rid of it all.' In five years, you're not going to have the option. You're always going to be on. Your car's going to be on. Your belt buckle's going to be on. Your shoes are going to be on. We need to talk to our kids so that when they get out of our house they don't decide 'Woo Hoo! I'm free now! I can do whatever I want!' We want them to learn and follow our example by putting restrictions on our kids and ourselves so that one day they realize, 'Yeah, I can't play that much, I've got to back-off on this and can avoid the bigger problems of technology.'"

CHAPTER 2

Why Guidelines are Important

The foremost expert on technology guidelines is Cris Rowan. She is a well-known speaker and author to teachers, parents, and therapists throughout North America and China. Her expertise is in sensory integration, learning attention, fine motor skills, and the impact of technology on children's neurological development. Cris and I both help parents on a daily basis as they deal with the challenges of life and have both been in the trenches with awesome parents who are facing some unimaginable difficulties.

The first time I learned about Cris was when I read her article in The Huffington Post, "10 Reasons Why Handheld Devices Should be Banned for Children Under the Age of 12".[28] It was a surprising headline to me, since for months I had seen parents ignoring this advice. I'd been with thousands of families at conferences all summer, and almost every young child I saw had a handheld device.

Can you ban technology for children under twelve? The reasons are clearly explained in the previous chapter, but boundaries must be clearly defined. Cris shares the "Technology Use Guidelines for Children and Youth" developed by a panel of experts. With contribution from the American Academy of Pediatrics and the

Canadian Pediatric Society, the guidelines were developed by Cris Rowan, Dr. Andrew Doan, neuroscientist and author of *Hooked on Games*, and Dr. Hilarie Cash, Director of reSTART Internet Addiction Recovery Program and author of *Video Games and Your Kids*. Health professionals and education professionals, who see this push for digital device use by very young children, loved the article. However, many parents were upset about the word "banned" in her article.

The guidelines for technology are simple and clear and can be used by every family.

Technology Use Guidelines for Children and Youth

Developmental Age	How Much	Non-Violent TV	Handheld devices	Non-Violent Video Games	Violent Video games	Online Violent Video Games or Pornography
0 - 2 Years	none	never	never	never	never	never
3 - 5 Years	1 hour a day	✓	never	never	never	never
6 - 12 Years	2 hours a day	✓	never	never	never	never
13 - 18 Years	2 hours a day	✓	✓	limit to 30 minutes a day	limit to 30 minutes a day	never

Please contact Cris Rowan at info@zonein.ca for additional information. © Zone'in

Technologic: How to Set Logical Technology Boundaries and Stop the Zombie Apocalypse

- For ages 0-2, children should not use technology at all.
- For ages 3-5, children can use technology for up to one hour a day of completely non-violent, prosocial TV (which means there are no characters trying to hurt each other). There should be no gaming or handheld devices at all.
- For ages 6-12, children can spend up to two hours per day watching non-violent TV. There should be no handheld devices at all.
- Teenagers 13 to 18 should engage in no more than two hours per day of personal technology use, and can start using handheld devices. Video games should be limited to 30 minutes per day; no online violent games should be allowed.

Cris' Counsel

"There is a certain degree of alarm by the health and education professionals, but parents are largely kept in the dark. I don't think the media is doing a great job in educating parents regarding the detrimental effects of tech."

Families are seeing soaring rates of aggression, defiance, and deviance in children due to violent video game content. Studies have shown that pro-social content in games can result in positive, pro-social behavior, which means good games can lead to good behavior.[29] However, video games can be addictive whether they're violent or non-violent. Non-violent video games are still immersive. There's also a social aspect, so kids can team together, which has an attraction. It's the addictive quality of video games that should guide you to limit exposure to them.

Each child is unique, of course, and some kids have difficulty handling 30 minutes each day and might do better restricted to 20 minutes. Watch for behavior changes after they finish playing games. If their behavior is difficult to manage, then you may want to decrease the duration of time they're playing.

(Not-so-Fun) Facts about Video Games:

1) Violent video games involve fighting and killing, which can make children aggressive and defiant[30]
2) Video games in general over-stimulate children, causing attention deficit disorder[31]
3) Video games keep kids from moving, causing obesity, which can lead to diabetes[32]
4) Video games isolate children, robbing them of much needed human connection and touch, resulting in anxiety, sadness, and tantrums[33]
5) Video games keep children indoors, resulting in problems paying attention and learning[34]

These technology guidelines should affect your views on education. Public schools, private schools, and home educators should keep an eye on technology use guidelines and how they fit in overall education plans. You may be concerned about all the hours children spend on schoolwork using technology each day. It can easily add up to two or more hours per day! Cris calls technology used for educational purposes EdTech or "digital broccoli" (her colleague Andy Doan's term), something that children need. Of course, children need a balance of healthy activity and technology, and you don't want all their educational experiences to be online. If your children are in school, keep an open discussion with their teachers so you know what they are doing each day. If you're a homeschool parent, ensure your child is getting what they need to grow and succeed, and limit technology in your homeschool day.

Cris' Counsel

"Parents with young children should avoid online games and technology in general while kids are awake."

It is fine to talk about guidelines for children, but how about guidelines for parents? What limits should you impose on yourself? Children need a lot of love and attention. They need to get outside and play. They need to have their friends over and enjoy play dates. They need to help you in the kitchen. These are important skill-building, social-building, and relationship-building activities. You need to be present and involved with your children, not their technology. These days, parents are attaching to their devices and detaching from their children. Children will substitute an unhealthy attachment to gadgets for their healthy attachment to parents. Be there for your children to make sure they are engaging in healthy activity and are properly supervised.

Lee's Lessons

"Watching a football game, we were shocked by a constant barrage of technology ad after technology ad. These commercials taught parents that they should put handheld devices into their babies' hands. Amazingly, they depicted young children, six months old through twenty-four months old using handheld devices, implying it was beneficial for the children. You need to be aware of the pressure being applied by marketers."

Commercials encourage parents to purchase technological devices and ignore reasonable technology guidelines. Companies spend millions of dollars marketing tech gadgets directly to parents of young children, trying to convince them that the devices are important, ubiquitous, and desirable.[35]

Technology interferes with learning. Today, young children are much better at using digital devices than tying their shoelaces. An interesting study was conducted by an optical specialist in Britain, to see if screen time was causing vision problems for children.[36] The study found that a surprising 30% of two to four-year-olds owned a tablet and were spending an average of more than five hours on digital devices each day! The situation here in the U.S. is similar, where a recent study by Common Sense Media found that over a third of children under the age of two play on their parents' smartphones, and a fifth of third graders have their own smartphones. These numbers are rising every year.

The time spent on digital devices cuts into learning through free play and reading together. Today's children can't tell time without looking at digital devices. This may predict a large societal problem as children grow older. Technology seems to be everywhere, even in education, in all its forms, public school, private school, and homeschool alike. Children face this technology constantly in their day-to-day living and learning.[37]

Cris' Counsel

"We've been sold a line of goods saying these technology gadgets are great for your kid, that they will make them successful and bright, and competent, and challenged. There isn't any research backing that at all. As far as I'm concerned, using technology with young children may be the biggest experiment in human history."

Face the Problem

CHAPTER 3

Eleven Long-term Consequences of Excessive Technology Use

Long-term, serious consequences of excessive technology use are recognized by medical science. Internet gaming disorder is now mentioned in the appendix of the American Psychiatric Association Diagnostic and Statistical Manual (DSM-5) as a condition that requires more research.[38] Excessive technology use has become such a problem that now it's mentioned in the same book that lists alcoholism as a psychiatric condition.

Consider these eleven long-term consequences of excessive technology use.

1. Self-Esteem Problems
Facebook has been called a "significant public health threat" by psychiatrist Dr. Keith Ablow. People are increasingly being enveloped in the world of social media, and studies have shown that social media comparisons can cause feelings of loneliness or jealousy. Surprisingly, sharing photos on Facebook decreases intimacy and closeness in friendships. Studies show that the more young people use social media sites, the worse they feel and the less satisfied they are with their lives.[39] Lack of self-esteem may start by looking like a small problem but it can lead to emotional disorders further down the road: eating disorders, alcoholism, and drug abuse.

Social media sites may intentionally influence your feelings. Facebook manipulated user emotions for a scientific experiment, without the users' knowledge.[40] While social media may intrinsically lead to uncomfortable feelings, the company took a step further, trying to manipulate those feelings for the sake of science. Social media sites are the greatest human research lab ever created, because almost everybody accepts their terms and conditions without reading the details. This creates amazing possibilities. There's no need to get experiment participants to sign a consent form, because users previously agreed to the site's data use policy, which includes that your information can be used for research in the fine print. A team of Facebook data scientists constantly comes up with new ways to study human behavior through their social network.

Facebook's research found that emotions can be contagious. Smiling and laughing babies make you smile, and horrible news reports make you feel worse afterward. Social media can produce the same reactions. "When positive expressions were reduced, people produced fewer positive posts and more negative posts; when negative expressions were reduced, the opposite pattern occurred," the Facebook research team found. "These results indicate that emotions expressed by others on Facebook influence our own emotions, constituting experimental evidence for massive-scale contagion via social networks."

Manipulating feelings can have serious consequences. "Probably nobody was driven to suicide," one professor commented on social media in regards to the study. As you survey social media, remember that when you see positive posts online, you feel more positive. When you see negative posts, you feel more negative. When your friends post that they are struggling, you're more likely to comment and Facebook is more likely to show you that post. Interestingly, when Facebook randomly removed all the emotional posts from some users' newsfeeds, each of them wrote fewer status updates.

These companies may control the information, highlighting emotional posts if they decide you're not posting often enough.

2. Dementia and Deterioration of Cognitive Abilities
As technology does more of the thinking for you, you become less able to think for yourself. Without the practice of daily problem solving, you can experience a deterioration of cognitive ability. The effects of excessive technology use can be similar to the effects of a head injury, psychiatric illness, or dementia such as Alzheimer's. These days, people age 18 to 34 are more likely to forget what day it is and where they put their keys than the elderly! Young people even forget to take showers on more occasions than seniors do.

You may not have realized that these are issues young people are experiencing; it can be shocking. Those who rely on electronic devices often can't remember even important details of their daily lives. It's difficult to recognize if this is happening to you and see that you are thinking less clearly and have reduced cognitive abilities.

Cris' Counsel
"When I was in China, I was speaking to corporate owners about productivity. Adults are having difficulties being productive, remembering, and concentrating. Cognitive function is declining the more you use devices."

You may notice that your ability to navigate is diminished with a GPS in the car. Once you give your brain permission to stop thinking about something (such as navigation), that portion of the brain begins to atrophy. "Use it or lose it" applies to every area of your brain that you hand over to technology. Consider your own spelling skills since the advent of spell-check! An article in Psychology Today, "Your Smartphone May Be Making You ... Not Smart" by

Susan Krauss Whitbourne, Ph.D., supports this contention. She states, "Research on technological tools suggests that offloading our mental functions to these electronic devices could cause our brains to go soft." It's not just calculators anymore; we even become used to driving to familiar locations in our own hometowns using navigation technology![41]

3. Under-developed Brain
The consequences of technology go beyond dementia or imitation of an aging brain. It can also slow the growth and development aspect of the young brain, as young people increasingly rely on technology instead of on their own thought processes. A heavy technology user is likely to develop the left side of the brain, leaving the right side of their brain less used over time, resulting in an under-developed brain. Your neural pathways are not stimulated when you let computers think for you.

Experts from South Korea are concerned because they have noticed a surge in teenagers with poor memory skills. This deterioration in thinking and cognitive ability is more commonly seen in people who suffer from head injuries or psychiatric illnesses. "Over-use of smartphones and game devices hampers the balanced development of the brain," says Byun Gi-won, a doctor from the Balance Brain Center in Seoul.[42] Teenagers have become so reliant on digital technology they are no longer able to remember everyday, simple details, such as their phone numbers. This is especially concerning with the increasing amount of technology used in education these days.

4. Memory and Concentration Damage
The right side of the brain is linked with concentration and memory. As people concentrate less and remember less information, this portion of the brain can deteriorate from lack of use. Information overload, which occurs easily in this technological age, isolates pieces of

information, making it hard to see the big picture and more difficult to remember. As you browse online, you click on what you see and lose the larger scope of what you are viewing. But it's more than forgetting what website you are on, or what you were searching for online. Now people use the internet as their brain's external hard drive. You have technology to store all the information you need, so you don't need to retain it in your brain. You can quickly search for what you need, or store information digitally to retrieve later. You may have a more difficult time remembering things because you don't have to remember. With less practice remembering, you remember less.

Distraction also affects memory profoundly. Some individuals talk with pride about their multi-tasking abilities, but the research is clear, multi-tasking makes it more difficult to learn and to accomplish tasks.[43] While you may feel as if you are doing two things at once when multi-tasking, this is not what scientific studies show. Instead, multi-tasking is like flipping a switch from one subject to another, with each subject distracting from the previous subject, in a constant stream of distraction. Teachers and professors witness this daily. Once a student opens their laptop, cell phone, or tablet, they remember little of what goes on in the classroom. Distraction has a negative impact on memory. Thinking is hard work – you have to concentrate. If you are distracted, you will learn less and act more like an elderly person who isn't thinking as clearly. Young people voluntarily experience these memory and concentration problems when they overuse technology, but it's not always an insignificant problem. An article in The Atlantic says, "Google is making students stupid"[44] because they are offloading their menial brain tasks to computers, robbing an entire generation of basic mental abilities.

Nicholas Carr, in *The Glass Cage: Automation and Us*,[45] demonstrates the consequences within specific groups over time. Older generations of Inuit hunters in northern Canada could track caribou deftly, simply through observing changes in the wind, snowdrift patterns, the location of the stars, and the behavior of surrounding animals. In recent years, young hunters have begun riding snowmobiles to hunt, using GPS units. Their reliance on GPS makes them reckless as they lose track of important details of their surroundings. Some will speed onto thin ice, or go over cliffs. When a GPS unit fails (often due to frozen batteries), these young hunters are vulnerable because they can't find their way like their elders before them.

Closer to home and more alarming, medical doctors now rely on software that helps them make medical decisions. Sometimes this leads to overlooking patients' subtle symptoms or even outright dismissing the correct diagnosis because it's unlikely. Commercial airline pilots are so used to using their guidance systems that when emergencies occur, they can forget they need to perform simple course corrections. As you increasingly rely on technology, you become less adaptive to your environment.

5. Video Game Addiction
Addiction is a persistent, compulsive dependence on a behavior or substance, a strong and harmful need to regularly have something or do something. When a person is addicted to video games, they willingly forego sleep, food, and human contact in order to feed their need, and may indulge in gaming for ten to twenty hours each day (or more). Video game addiction is a huge problem, particularly for college students. If you have young children, it is critical to pay close attention, and be prepared. If you have high schoolers, it is critical to teach your children about it. Children eventually grow up and go to college, so you must be able to meet this concern with wisdom.

While common in high school, this problem is rampant in colleges. An anonymous writer from Inside Higher ED wrote about the experience they had with their own child's video game addiction.

Technologic: How to Set Logical Technology Boundaries and Stop the Zombie Apocalypse

> "Until the academic warning letter from my son's college arrived home last December 23rd following his fall freshman term, he assured us that he was getting Bs in his classes. Confronted with this letter, he broke down in tears, admitted that he spent most of the last half of the semester playing an online computer game, and didn't attend the final weeks of classes nor even sit for his exams. An activity that started out in high school for fun and as a coping strategy for stress had hijacked his brain, and he lost control. He was addicted to video games – as are nearly 2 million other U.S. college students."[46]

Game designers purposefully make their games addictive, creating and expanding the problem. These companies want people to become addicted. Creating compulsive behavior will sell more of their products; they have a financial investment in getting your children addicted to video games. When you combine intentional psychological programming by designers, with a child's predilection for gaming, and add it to those who are more prone to addiction of any kind, it creates the perfect storm of true addiction.

Imitating the tobacco industry marketing strategy from decades ago, computer games are now designed to hook addicts at a young age. As early as 1939, real cigarette pack designs were being used on candy cigarettes. In the 1960s and '70s, candy cigarettes were widely available in the candy aisle of the grocery store and every corner store. Tobacco companies teamed up with candy companies, wanting young children to think it was "cool" to smoke cigarettes. In a comparable partnership, today's game makers team up with toy manufacturers to create tiny Halo, Minecraft and World of Warcraft characters for toys such as Lego sets and action figures targeting the five to ten age group. The Inside Higher Ed article also mentions one gaming industry executive's confession at a 2010 conference, "We have to bring them in and keep them addicted and make them keep playing."

Tracy Markle, founder of Collegiate Coaching Services, has seen a huge rise in pathological computer gaming among her young adult clients:

> "In our initial assessments on new male clients, 75% have some level of computer gaming and/or Internet abuse issue that contributes to the original presenting problems such as poor academic performance, difficulty concentrating, and social anxieties."

The problem of gaming excess may begin as early as elementary or middle school and become a big problem in high school, only to increase to a full addiction when children attend college. You must recognize the long-term consequences, and guide your young adults through this challenging maze of technology. It's important to think about the big picture for your children and teens, and not lose sight of it as they grow older.

6. Lower Academic Performance
It is clear that excessive gaming is linked to lower academic performance.[47] The reasons vary, from simple to complex. Of course, more time gaming means less time studying – a simple cause-and-effect result. Students also often care about playing games more than learning. But technology use also creates complicated challenges for educators. Excessive use of technology makes it more difficult to learn. Changes in the brain affect cognitive abilities, making it harder for your child to learn in the long run.

This isn't restricted to high school and college. Career performance is also affected by technology abuse. Children drop out of high school and college, and adults are fired from their jobs.

> **Lee's Lessons**
> "One parent I know confessed that her gainfully employed child was fired for repeatedly using social media during business hours, even after multiple warnings, as if he was unable to control his own behavior."

Staying focused while surrounded by technology can be difficult, so teachers and professors have begun to ban devices in class. In the article, "Why Clay Shirky Banned Laptops, Tablets and Phones from His Classroom,"[48] a professor who teaches a college class on social media explains that he originally allowed devices in class, but his rules have changed. He requires students to stay focused, with no devices in class unless required due to the nature of the assignment.

Distraction by technology in the classroom hinders classroom learning for everyone nearby, similar to the effect of second-hand smoking. If the person next to you uses technology, research shows their technology use can affect you.[49] The evidence is clear: multi-tasking has a negative effect on the quality of work done, especially for the kind of work asked of college students or newly hired employees. Using laptops in the classroom not only hinders learning for the laptop user, but also everybody in their proximity.

7. Mental Health Disorders
Mental health disorders related to excessive technology can include depression, anxiety, attention deficit hyperactive disorder, and social phobias. The relationship between technology and mental illness is being studied on college campuses, where a variety of

internet-related disorders are treated. This is an expensive problem, because each student with a disorder must be treated.

Mental health disorders are more costly to treat than physical disorders, and society will bear the increasing weight of these costs as more people suffer from these symptoms of over-use. College costs will increase, as colleges have to handle these conditions in their campus health centers. Students with addictions are less able to control their own behavior and may become non-compliant regarding treatment – they don't want treatment because they don't want to stop their addictive behavior.

Many serious mental health disorders pop up for the first time when a child becomes an adult, between the ages of 18 to 25. Young people may display symptoms of serious mental health disorders, appearing to have schizophrenia or bipolar disorder. Technology may be causing these symptoms in some young adults. Therefore, when symptoms of mental health disorders pop up, it can be difficult to distinguish whether it is a brain issue caused by an intrinsic condition, or whether it's the second-hand result of excessive technology use.

Spending too much time online can cause symptoms of mental illness in younger children as well. Government health advisors at Public Health England warn that loneliness, depression, anxiety, low self-esteem, and heightened aggression are some of the possible issues faced, even by young children who overuse the internet. One in ten children now have a mental health issue, and one third of teenagers feel "low, sad or down" at least once a week. The risk of mental illness is present when children spend only a few hours a day online, but the problem becomes even more striking when children spend more than four hours a day in front of screens. The report states:

"The evidence suggests a 'dose-response' relationship, where each additional hour of viewing increases children's likelihood of experiencing socio-economic problems, and the risk of lower self-esteem."[50]

This study is particularly significant for you as parents. It's important to limit technology use, keeping it to less than two hours a day even if your child is an older teenager. If you are not able to set technology boundaries and your children get over four hours a day in front of any screen, they will face more potential problems.

8. Increased Suicide Risk

The depression and anxiety disorders caused by technology overuse can cause increased suicide risk. The possibility of suicide is also related to escapism; people who overuse technology may be trying to escape from some aspect of their lives. Instead of escaping through alcohol or drugs to numb the pain, they escape into the digital world, which is more socially acceptable.

Technology sometimes encourages suicidal behavior, making matters worse. As depression, anxiety, and escapism are becoming more problematic due to technology abuse, some video games actively encourage suicide. It's easy for children and teens to stumble upon sites that openly encourage suicide as a solution to problems.

You may not know your child is depressed and at increased risk of suicide. Only 16% of children regularly speak to their parents about what they do online. If you are concerned, speak to your children. Ask your child if they feel suicidal or as if they might self-harm. Research shows that asking about suicide does not increase suicide risk, and it can give you the parent the information you need to reach out and get help. Discussing it will not cause them to attempt suicide. Asking them about it will instead reduce their anxiety. Don't hesitate to ask your children. If you need help, you can contact the National Suicide Prevention Hotline in the U.S. (1-800-273-8255). To learn more about suicide prevention, please go to the National Suicide Prevention Lifeline website at www.suicidepreventionlifeline.org.

9. Escape from Real Life
Teenagers may use the internet to escape from daily life. As they grow and mature, some teens feel stressed by the adult world and prefer not to grow up. Even while they appear mature and confident at times, they may prefer escapism. They want to be grown up in some ways, such as increasing independence by driving, but are terrified by the other aspects of adulthood.

To avoid increasing responsibilities, some teens are pulled into the virtual world. Often this is a world filled with video games or social media. Boys tend to be more involved in video games, whereas girls tend to be more involved in social media. Video games can be violent or non-violent - it's not only Call of Duty or World of Warcraft that sucks people in. In the world of social media, it's not always about Facebook. It can be Snapchat, Instagram, Twitter, Pinterest, or the latest social media fad – any one of them can be used to escape from real life.

The PBS video, "Growing Up Online,"[51] describes an extreme, real life example of escapism. A girl named Jessica secretly created an online alter ego, "Autumn," without her parents' knowledge. In real life, Jessica is a young woman who is picked on and feels insecure; her alter ego is a sexy Goth model who dresses up in lingerie and strikes poses for the whole world to see on the internet. It took a long time for Jessica's parents to find out; someone from their daughter's school notified them. They were shocked because they had no idea this could possibly have been going on. Initially, they punished their daughter but then decided to allow her to continue, this time with their consent. Consent will only compound this problem, because developing an alter ego can indicate a problem with personality development.

In another example of escapism, a young man playing a video game completely lost touch with reality in one online Call of Duty game gone awry. When the game ended, the loser of the game made a prank call to police, posing as his opponent, claiming, "I just killed my mother and I might shoot more people."[52] This phony call to authorities put into motion a massive police response and the S.W.A.T. team descended on a Long Island home. The teen who made the call wanted to get back at his opponent for beating him at the game. While the prank call was serious, and the police activity concerning, what was even more shocking was the response by the winner of the Call of Duty game. The teen winner was still engrossed in the game when the S.W.A.T. team arrived. His mother and brother met police outside the house and assured them that his mother was in fact still alive. It took the police 20 minutes to get the teen's attention and get him out of the house to reconfirm the hoax. He was so engrossed in the game that he didn't notice the noise of the helicopters and police surrounding his home.

You must be involved and aware of what your children are doing online. You must set boundaries, and check what your children are doing on their devices. It's important to become involved in what your children are doing and learn more about it, whether it is video games, social media, or other online activities.

10. Depression and Sadness
Depression and sadness seem pervasive among young people. Technology use can produce these symptoms, especially when you have devices in the bedroom. It's important to keep all digital devices out of the bedroom. It doesn't matter if your children like to use them as alarm clocks, because there are inexpensive alternatives that will not cause problems. Young people need sleep

more than they need to have a phone or digital device in their room. Make sure your children "unplug" an hour prior to going to bed so their brains can slow down and allow them to fall asleep normally.

Teens at risk of depression may reach out to others online and tell their friends, but friends don't have any idea how to help. It's important for you as parents to recognize what your children are going through and talk to them.

11. Digital or Internet Addiction
Addiction is a habitual or compulsive involvement in an activity. It is being enslaved to a habit or to something that is psychologically or physically habit-forming, to the extent that stopping it causes severe trauma. When a person spends most of their time online, they may become addicted to the behavior. Excessive internet use or use of devices interferes with activities of daily living and with social relationships of all kinds.

> *Lee's Lessons*
> "We went to the theater one night, and most of the audience was still seated when we came back in after intermission. They were all checking their phones in silence, not talking about the play, the performance, or the actors. The entire audience was on their phones, checking obsessively."

One parent shares the first sign of serious digital addiction they noticed in their child. He came home from college for a visit and proudly announced he had achieved a high global ranking in the video game, Rainbow Unicorn Attack. It sounds like such a harmless game, and it probably is, but this teen was playing excessively. Proudly proclaiming he was in the top 100 in the world for this video game, he failed to mention he was receiving an "incomplete" grade for every single college class, jeopardizing his graduation. Simple games played online can cause serious problems and lead to serious digital addiction, leaving people no longer in full control of their behavior. His compulsive need for the game was destroying his life, because all he wanted was more gaming time.

Internet and digital addiction can go far beyond video gaming, taking many forms. A person can become addicted to seemingly harmless online behavior, such as playing online word games, to much more serious-looking activities that have devastating effects on families. Internet addiction can include obsessive gambling, shopping, and pornography. It can also appear more benign; simply reading fiction or technical writing online can be addictive.

Pornography addiction has serious consequences, and it's important for you to become aware of the issues, so you can help your children. In a talk about pornography addiction, Gary Wilson explains that the human brain is not able to handle the hyper-stimulation of today's internet enticements.[53] Parents must be on their guard, because according to Wilson, most boys search for internet pornography by the age of ten. He believes that of all the activities on the internet, pornography has the most potential to become addictive, and pornography addiction has become widespread.

Parent's Perspective

♡ "We have run into issues with our son and his girlfriend ... girls are very bold and we have been shocked by the pictures and suggestive content sent to him. He also was sexted by a male student in his school. Our phone company would only remove this child's information for a fee. Don't forget you can never 'unsee' things ... that's something

> we have explained to our kids - once you see it, you store it to memory. That has helped somewhat, even in choosing movies and so forth."
>
> ~Judith

According to Wilson, internet pornography addiction is even causing an epidemic of youthful erectile dysfunction. The reason you see so many commercials about ED on TV is that it has become an issue even among young people because of their addiction to internet pornography. This is the only symptom that seems to get the attention of young porn viewers, and it's worth remembering this when discussing the harmful effects of pornography on teenagers. It is difficult for teenagers, and even adults, to understand the risks and how it can affect them. The results of internet pornography addiction can affect a young person's future marriage relationship.

> **Parent's Perspective**
> "I want to ask the parents of boys to add that it's not respectful of women and not normal. I worry a generation is growing up and thinks porn is normal human sexual behavior."
>
> ~Stephanie

Cell phone addiction is particularly concerning these days, because almost everybody owns a cell phone. It can be difficult for you to tell when your cell phone dependence becomes an addiction. You carry them around with you all day long! With cell phones in particular, the compulsion to talk and text can affect anyone. Sadly, people use their digital devices to text while driving. Even in areas where it's illegal, people still use cell phones while driving. The results of texting and driving can be dire, but even responsible adults have trouble controlling their behavior, and people of all ages have been killed due to collisions caused by texting and driving.

According to a study, approximately 60% of college students admit they suffer from some form of internet addiction.[54] The cell phone activities that produce the most addictive associations were not surfing the internet or playing games, but checking social media accounts. The test for addiction is if the cell phone moves from being a helpful tool to one that undermines the user's well-being and the well-being of others. In your daily life, you can see obsessive or excessive cell phone use causing conflict inside the classroom with professors, at work, and at home with family members.

CHAPTER 4

Twelve Symptoms of Serious Technology Abuse

Internet addiction is not always related to pornography or violent video games. It can be related to something as benign as social media involvement, cell phone use, texting, or reading online to excess. Almost anything online can result in addiction, which makes it difficult to identify. One young man experienced digital addiction requiring in-patient treatment. He was addicted to reading and writing fan fiction stories online. It didn't involve anything bad, but he was involved in fan fiction to the point of physical and emotional illness. How can you tell if your teenager has serious technology issues?

Addiction means a person is willing to forego sleep, food, and human contact to feed their technology needs, sometimes staying online for 10 to 20 hours a day or more. The biggest indicator of addiction is when a person uses technology to escape an aspect of their daily life. Watch for this one big factor that can help you determine if excessive use will become an addiction. This is when their technology use is more likely to cause severe problems.

As technology changes and evolves, any new technology can be addictive, and it's not limited to cell phones, portable devices, and personal computers. One 31-year-old man was treated for the world's first case of Google Glass addiction.[55] He wore this device, a computer in the form of eyeglasses, for 18 hours a day and took it off only to sleep and bathe. He checked into a treatment center for alcoholism, the US Navy Substance Abuse program, which requires all patients to abstain from drugs, sex, alcohol, and cigarettes for 35 days. The program also takes away all electronic devices at the door and they confiscated the Google Glass. The doctors quickly noticed that the man would frequently and involuntarily lift his right hand and tap his temple – a motion used to activate the display of Google Glass. He exhibited the classic symptoms of withdrawal: frustration, irritability, aggression, and cravings. His addiction also left him with short-term memory problems.

He was "going through withdrawal from his Google Glass," Dr. Andrew Doan, head of addictions and resilience research at the Navy's Substance Abuse and Recovery Program and co-author of the recently released paper on the patient, says. "[The patient] said the Google Glass withdrawal was greater than the alcohol withdrawal he was experiencing." After 35 days, the patient reported an improvement in his mood and short-term memory, and was no longer making involuntary movements. Upon his release, he was referred to a 12-step alcohol abuse program, the theory being that all addictions are similar.

No matter how technology changes in the future, with new social media or new devices, the science and symptoms of addiction are the same and the possibility for technology addiction will remain the same as well. One young person had an active social life: dancing every weekend, swimming, soccer, fencing, judo, politics, public speaking, and campus activities. Once technology addiction set in, he changed so much that it seemed as if he had a personality transplant. Technology was the only activity left in his life. Learn the symptoms of technology addiction so you can help and guide your loved ones.

The 12 Symptoms of Internet Abuse
The following list of symptoms of internet abuse was put together by Dr. Hilarie Cash, PhD, at www.NetAddictionRecovery.com. Keep in mind that addiction doesn't mean any particular kind of technology; it can be seemingly benign.

Warning Signs and Symptoms[56]
Three or four yes answers suggests serious issues. Answering five or more with a yes suggests an addiction.

1. Increasing Amounts of Time Spent with Technology
Gaming or social media becomes addictive. Spends little time with people in real life.

2. Failed Attempts to Control their Own Behavior
Expressing anger and sadness. Wants to change, but seems unable to change behavior. May agree compliantly, but then are back at it when your back is turned.

3. Heightened Euphoria While Using Technology
Heightened sense of euphoria while involved in computer and internet activities. Has to get to the next level in the video game. Can't miss anything on social media. This can almost look physically like drug abuse. May have dilated pupils, excessive sweating, and tremulousness.

4. Craving More Time Online
Always needing more time on the computer and internet. Getting to the next level in video games takes more and more time. A teenage boy may crave technology more than food or want to use it more than joining you at the dinner table, and eat unhealthy convenience foods to have more time to consume digital media.

5. Neglecting Family and Friends
Rejects the company of family or friends for digital media. Could have difficulty engaging in family activities, or flat out refuse to join in with others. It's difficult to determine if this is normal teenage angst. Look closely and determine if they perceive technology as more enjoyable than being with their friends.

6. Restlessness When Not Online
Feels restless when not engaged in online activity. ADHD symptoms can appear. Can't sit still to watch a family movie. Going on a hike with family may cause anxiety. They may do fine at a family function for a short period of time, but become more anxious as time goes on and they become more eager to return to their computer or device.

7. Being Dishonest About Technology Use
Lies about sites visited, or lies about length of time on computer or devices. May be sneaking computer usage. One parent found his son hiding in the laundry room at five in the morning because he had been sneaking some computer use the entire night.

8. Interfering with Job or School Performance
Technology use makes it impossible to complete job or school demands on time. More time spent on digital media means less time studying. May be sneaking time at work to engage in social media or online gaming. Has less interest in going out and doing work or volunteer work. Is failing school, has incomplete classes, is withdrawing from classes, and is not finishing schoolwork.

9. Feelings of Guilt and Shame
Feeling guilty, ashamed, anxious, or depressed as a result of behavior. Feels bad about lying regarding social media use or length of time online. The guilt and shame are cyclical – the more guilt and shame felt, the more technology is used to escape the feelings, so it can snowball.

10. Changes in sleep patterns

Texts or gaming throughout the night leads to sleep interruptions and insomnia. Technology in the bedroom can make this worse.

11. Changes in Physical Health

People experience huge physical changes from head to toe as part of their affliction. Physical changes such as weight gain from eating unhealthy, hand-held junk food, to weight loss from not eating at all. Backaches, headaches, carpal tunnel syndrome, and other repetitive stress injuries also develop, from spending too long at the keyboard, texting, or manipulating the mouse or game controller. Illnesses from immobility or circulatory problems from sitting for lengthy periods can occur, similar to what people experience on planes when they develop blood clots from sitting too long.

Ophthalmologists are concerned by excessive use of digital screens, noticing a huge increase in problematic dry, scratchy eyes caused by staring at screens; when you do a lot of screen reading rather than book reading, you tend to blink less. When you don't blink your eyes often enough, they get too dry. If your eyes feel as dry and scratchy as a sand dune and your vision improves when you blink, you may have dry-eye syndrome. This used to be primarily a condition that affected women, brought on by hormonal changes during menopause. Because the entire population is constantly staring at screens, it's become an equal opportunity ailment. "Now the dry eye is almost epidemic," says Dr. Stephanie Marioneaux, "In today's world when people are so transfixed with tablets, phones, cable TV without commercials, you're not blinking."[57] Dry eyes may not be one of the major consequences of excessive technology use, but it's interesting to note that it affects people physically as well as psychologically.

12. Withdrawing From Other Pleasurable Activities

The desire to spend time on digital media means less desire to enjoy activities with friends and family. Becomes less interested in anything that is not digital media and no longer engages in activities they used to enjoy. This can take many forms:

"I'm bored"
"This is what I love to do"
"This is my passion"
"It's the only thing that is fun"

> ### Parent's Perspective
> "Recently heard that the 'alert' sound of a text sends dopamine through the brain, as a reward, and it gives us a feeling of pleasure, much like how we would feel when we got a letter in the mail (in the old days). This dopamine dose begins to build dependence and when we hear the alerts again, it's almost an irresistible urge to respond and read it. Wow!"
>
> ~a mom

Addiction can be extreme and life threatening for the addicted person, but the addiction can hurt others as well. A manslaughter case against Kim Yoo-chul and Choi Mi-sun inspired Valerie Veatch to create the documentary, "Love Child."[58] This South Korean couple was so immersed in a massive multiplayer online game (MMO) that they let their child starve to death, as they carefully raised and nurtured a virtual child in the online game. This film addresses the problem faced by nations across the globe as daily lives become more integrated with the internet. This is how addiction usually ends, not how it begins – it begins slowly.

CHAPTER 5

The Impact of Technology on the Developing Child

Children are growing and developing the sensory, motor, and attachment systems. Their bodies cannot accommodate the sedentary, frenzied, random nature of technology. The increasing use of technology by developing children has caused an increase of physical, psychological, and behavior disorders. Child obesity and diabetes are epidemic in both Canada and the U.S., and experts believe this may be related to technology overuse. Children are increasingly diagnosed with ADHD, autism, coordination disorder, developmental delays, unintelligible speech, learning difficulties, sensory processing disorder, anxiety, depression, and sleep disorders. These are associated with technology overuse, and all are increasing at an alarming rate. As children rely more on technology for the majority of their play, their creativity and imagination are limited. They do not experience the normal challenges their bodies need to achieve optimal sensory and motor development.

Cris Rowan is a well-known author and speaker in the field of sensory integration, learning attention, fine motor skills, and the impact of technology on children's neurological development.[59] She promotes the concept of Balanced Technology Management (BTM) to help parents raise children who will develop optimally, behave appropriately, and have the ability to pay attention and learn. Parents must balance technology with healthy activity and provide children with four basic factors: movement, touch, connection, and nature.

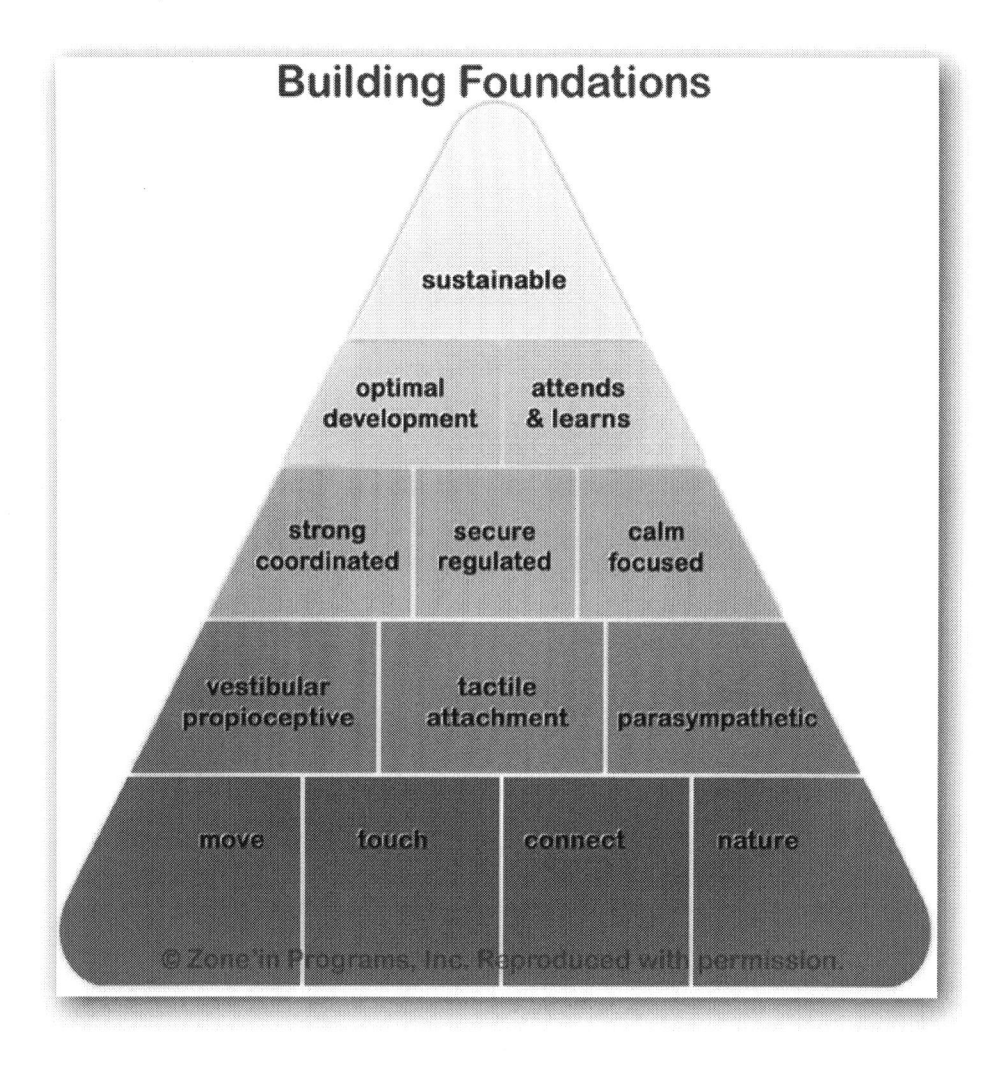

Building Foundations

- sustainable
- optimal development | attends & learns
- strong coordinated | secure regulated | calm focused
- vestibular propioceptive | tactile attachment | parasympathetic
- move | touch | connect | nature

© Zone'in Programs, Inc. Reproduced with permission.

Movement
Movement is a critical ingredient in childhood. It's vital for the cardiovascular system. Exercise prevents obesity and diabetes. When

Technologic: How to Set Logical Technology Boundaries and Stop the Zombie Apocalypse

you move, you stimulate two systems. First is the vestibular system, which enables a child to build a strong core. You see a child who is able to coordinate their muscles, coordinate their upper and lower body, their right side to left side, their eyes to the hand, and the eye to the eye. Whenever you stimulate the vestibular system by taking the child off their center, then you are building core and motor coordination. Increasingly, you're seeing what Cris terms "floppy kids." They're weak in the trunk and have great difficulty coordinating anything. This can have an effect not only on the athletics or health of a child, but also on literacy. Children need to be able to coordinate eye-to-hand for printing and eye-to-eye for reading.

Second, movement stimulates the muscles and joints. This activates the proprioceptive system, which enables the child to refine movement. Movement is important, not only for health but also for attainment of literacy and to play competitive sports. Past generations of kids were always out in the neighborhood after school and on weekends, climbing trees and playing ball. You had swings, slides, and merry-go-rounds to play on. Much of this play equipment has been banished as too dangerous, or at least, scaled down and slowed down. Play equipment has been made more safe, but much less fun. On school playgrounds, kids aren't allowed to play in the trees. In the winter, they often aren't allowed to play in the snow or make snowmen, for fear they will hurt each other with snowballs. They aren't allowed on the play equipment in the winter, for fear of slipping on ice. Today's children are not being provided with enough of this critical movement and stimulation that Cris recommends, to build a strong core with all its benefits.

Cris' Counsel

"Playground equipment is constantly being made safer – so much so that now they are barely challenging kids' motor systems at all."

Touch

Touch is so important for life. Affectionate, loving touch is a key ingredient for healthy brain development, and critically important for a child's physical and mental development. When babies are born in hospitals today, health professionals routinely teach parents the importance of skin-to-skin contact, especially to ensure breastfeeding success. Hospitals now focus on "The Golden Hour" directly after birth. For the first hour of baby's life, they remain skin-to-skin with their mother and all routine tests and procedures are delayed.

This skin-to-skin contact can be life saving for preemies! "Kangaroo Care" was first used in Bogota, Colombia in 1983. Premature babies, clad only in diapers, were placed on the bare skin of their parents' chests. The mortality rate fell at an incredible rate, from 70% to 30%. Today, Kangaroo Care is used in hospitals around the world. The effects of skin-to-skin contact can be dramatic. One mother, whose premature twin was pronounced dead after 20 minutes of trying to resuscitate him, held him skin-to-skin to say goodbye. After five minutes, he revived, and today, he and his twin sister are happy and healthy children.[60]

Affectionate touch is one big reason why pediatricians suggest zero technology use for children newborn to two years old. This is the time when the brain triples in size, not necessarily in the number of neurons, but connections between neurons. If you expose a newborn to two-year-old to an enriched environment, and view their brain in an MRI, you can see a huge area of the brain light up. The connections build an enriched brain. If the child's brain isn't stimulated in this area, they're not receiving attachment stimulation. Medical experts can see atrophy in this area of the brain. This causes all kinds of problematic behavior in children.

> **Cris' Counsel**
> "We're seeing touch deprivation, and the result is a child who is highly anxious. Anxiety is the fastest growing child mental illness today."

It's been common knowledge since the 1940s that if you don't touch children, they die. This is life-sustaining input that children need and people are not touching their children enough; touch deprivation is occurring, which causes anxiety. For children with anxiety, fear, and safety issues, therapists use a technique called deep pressure touch to lower cortisone and adrenaline levels. It works on the parasympathetic system to counteract the fright, fight, and flight response. The sympathetic charge helps children feel calm and more relaxed.

You need to give your kids a lot of touch. You can give your kids the deep pressure touch Cris says they need with a simple bear hug! The rough and tumble play between kids or your husband and the kids is terrific. Snuggle together on the couch or in their room before they go to bed every night and read a book. The skin is the largest organ of the body and it requires stimulation.

Connection

Human connection is vital for everyone at any age. You all know it's important. You've seen or heard about the effects of a lack of human connection on children in orphanages: attachment disorders, oppositional defiance disorder, and more. Attachment is formed between baby and parent, beginning in utero, and continues throughout a child's life. This attachment forms the child's ability to relate to others, even into adulthood.

Sadly, technology is getting in the way of human connection. Increasingly, kids are spending time on devices due to loneliness or a desire to escape what's happening in their lives. Connection can help them cope and help them feel safe.

When you're breastfeeding your baby, you are face-to-face, at the optimal distance for them to see you – it's the limit of their eyesight when they are a newborn – God's perfect design. You can look them in the eyes, face-to-face, and make that connection. This is why bottle-feeding parents are encouraged to hold their children while feeding them in a similar fashion, for the stimulation. As your child gets older and sits at the dinner table, you're engaged with the child, getting face-to-face time. But family meals at the dinner table aren't the norm anymore; the average American family eats out almost five times per week.[61] Walk into any restaurant and what do you see? Parents and children of all ages with their noses in digital devices. But it's such a critical time for them to be connecting as a family.

Cris has more to say about the effects of connection on children:

> "There's a term called co-regulation, the attachment formation between parent and child leads to self-regulation, which is that child's ability to control their energy states … to not have a tantrum when something's going wrong, to be able to wait in line, to be able to wait their turn, to be able to delay their gratification. In this world of immediacy and disconnection, we're seeing so many children having problems with self-regulation and tantrums. It's the most frequent reason kids get referred to me … even tantrums at the age of 12 and 13."

Tantrums at the age of 12 or 13 are not normal. It seems some kids only have a connection to technology. Kimberly has been taking exchange students into her home for over a dozen years. She told me that things have changed radically within that time. It used to be the only thing host parents had to worry about was a child spending too much time on the phone; now there are so many devices, it's a different world. One 14-year-old boy had a complete toddler-style meltdown in her home, pitching a crying and screaming fit on the floor in front of her bedroom when the family rule, "no devices in the bedroom" was enforced. Parents need to wake up to their children's needs for connection, or this can be the result.

Nature

Nature is a key ingredient for healthy children. Research indicates that green space restores the attention span, calms the senses, and increases the ability to learn. A study at the University of Illinois found that kids in the inner city had more problems with ADHD than rural kids did because children living outside the city have access to green space for about 20 minutes per day.[62] Nature not only has attention restorative benefits, but also activates all the senses to enhance multisensory learning ability. Participation in physical activity is even positively related to children's academic performance[63].

> ### Cris' Counsel
> "Children should be doing one class a day outside or one segment to their study should be outside. In addition, make sure they have some adequate play time outside."

Technology has a grave impact on the four critical factors of movement, touch, connection, and nature. Children with devices are sedentary. They're untouched and isolated from each other. They are indoors, or unaware of nature around them. Children are neglected in these four critical ways whenever they're handed devices.

Virtual Futures

TV	cellphone	internet

sedentary | isolated | neglected | overstumulated

| developmental delay / obesity | mental illnes / detached | ADHD / autism |

- diabetes
- stroke
- ♥ attack

- addicted
- violent
- perverted

- compulsive
- medicated
- illiterate

early death | no relationship | no job

unsustainable

© Zone'in Programs, Inc.
Reproduced with permission.

Children learn by example. They do not necessarily want digital devices, but they look at their moms and dads using devices, and they follow the example given to them. Immediately, their visual systems and brain structures become overstimulated with fast-paced media content. In Canada and the U.S., one third of children enter school developmentally delayed. Twenty-five percent are obese, and thirty percent of those go on to develop diabetes, making them more at-risk of early heart attack and stroke. Because children are neglected and isolated by the use of digital devices, a rise in mental illness is occurring through this detachment.

Many children are becoming addicted, violent, or aggressive. The pornography and violence embedded into video games can be horrendous. They are affecting and perverting young, developing brains. Because of the overstimulation and fast pace of media content, there's a rise in attention deficit disorder. Because of detachment, there are problems with autism directly related to overuse of technology.

Doctors respond to this crisis primarily though diagnosis and medication, rather than advising behavior changes. Children are assigned many adult diagnoses now. Cris reports that in Canada, one in seven children have a diagnosed mental illness. Twenty-seven years ago, the number was zero. She had no children in her caseload twenty-seven years ago with a diagnosed mental illness. Impulsivity is a result of the brain damage being done by fast-paced media, and illiteracy because of the motor coordination problems and difficulty with the eyes. She's seeing unsustainable children.

Cris' Counsel

"The ways we're raising, educating our kids with technology, are not resulting in a child who's going to grow up and have relationships and be able to move into an employment field and be socially-competent and able to do productive work. Our kids have never been sicker than they are today both mentally and physically."

CHAPTER 6

Technology in Education

The recent shift of child experiences from physical to digital has turned child development upside down. The research shows problems with excess technology in education, while schools continue to ask for more and more funding for technology.

Cris Rowan explains:

> "It's important to understand a little bit about how the brain develops. We can see the impact of technology on brain development. Children are born with their full complement of neurons. Neurons are like roads on a map. If I were to lay out a detailed map of say, British Columbia, you would see roads going everywhere. That's the way the child's brain is when they're born; they have all the roads in place. They form connections or synapses between neurons based on their environmental stimuli or lack thereof. The way those connections form is dependent on what we expose the child to. In an enriched environment, we're going to see a proliferation of synaptic connections. If they just engage in a lot of stimulus/response video games, texting, and other technology that does not require higher levels of thinking, they are only going to be developing those connections with lower brain functions.

Studies show that kids who game more than four to five hours per day are seeing a decrease in the size of their frontal lobes. It is as if the brain is pruning back what isn't being used. Recent studies show atrophy or shrinkage in the frontal lobes, both in the gray and the white matter. The white matter is the neurons that are doing the transmission and the synaptic connections. The frontal lobes are responsible for what we term 'executive function,' which is the ability of the individual to see the big picture, action and consequence, being able to critically think, memorize, concentrate, learn, and pay attention. Those are all functions we need our frontal lobes for, and this is why we're seeing soaring rates of ADHD and other learning disorders (in particular, anything that involves attention, memory, and concentration)."

Excessive technology in education will create a child who can't learn. This is the learning paradox. The more digital media they use, the less likely children are to learn. Consider each child as a unique individual, where some use technology a little, and others use it a lot. How much digital game or screen use do they have on board when they enter school around age six? If a child is already a heavy technology user, teachers might not be able to use technology to teach them. Contrast this child with a six-year-old who has had little exposure to technology, experience with a variety of other activities, and is highly social. This might be a child you can use educational technology with effectively.

There is no research that shows educational technology does anything other than entertain children, yet whole schools and nations are moving forward with a "one tablet per child" policy, requiring children use tablets for the curriculum. This educational shift is happening without evidence. Tablets have only been in existence for a few years. Accurate, adequate research isn't going to be available for another 10 to 15 years.

Technologic: How to Set Logical Technology Boundaries and Stop the Zombie Apocalypse

In his book, *The Glass Cage*, Nicholas Carr talks about the design of education technology being tech-centered, rather than human-centered. You may ask, "What can the tech do?" If the technology can do it, then it's added to the educational structure. You may assign everything you can to technology and as little as possible to the human. What people should be doing is centering education around human-centered designs. You should ask, "What are people good at?" Teachers are good at being humans; they're attachment figures providing important connection. They are providing touch and the human piece. In the absence of the teacher, you have no idea what the children are even learning. You may need to step back a bit, and proceed with caution. You should start looking seriously at it, asking yourself if this is education or merely a bunch of facts the kids aren't absorbing because they are displayed too quickly. Take a deep breath and start evaluating the usefulness and effectiveness of this path before moving forward.

The Research Regarding Technology in the Classroom

What does the research say about using technology in education, and how it affects learning? Cris Rowan put together a terrific collection of research on technology in education. See the "Zone'in Fact Sheet: A research review regarding the impact of technology on child development, behavior, and academic performance." A review of the research by Cris Rowan in her Zone'in Fact Sheet[64] reveals concerns in multiple areas and levels of education.

- **The more schools invest in technology, the less likely kids will pay attention and learn.** Schools are spending money on technology and it's backfiring. Recently, Canada dropped out of the top ten ranking on an international evaluation that tests reading, math, and science. The U.S. has dropped to number 27. Cris asks, "If all this technology that we're using is supposed to make our children more successful, then why isn't it doing that?"

- **Multi-tasking on a laptop distracts both the user and fellow students.** Participants who multitasked on a laptop during a lecture scored lower on the test compared to those who did not multitask. Participants who were in direct view of a multitasking peer scored lower on the test compared to those who were not. Multitasking on a laptop can be detrimental to comprehension of lecture content.
- **Technology in education is not evidence-based.** Schools are constantly discussing how important evidence-based education is, yet without any evidence regarding the efficacy of technology, whole school districts are moving rapidly toward virtual teaching. Devices are replacing teaching, and the teacher becomes a "moderator."
- **Print reading is superior to screen reading.** There are benefits to reading print text, rather than reading digital media text. A comparative study reports five distinct problems with screen reading:
  - Attention: clicking and scrolling disrupt attention and disturb mental appreciation
  - Comprehension: reader lacks both completeness and constituent parts
  - Memory: change in physical surroundings has a negative effect on memory
  - Learning: doesn't allow required time and mental exertion
  - Meaning: isn't a physical dimension, loss of totality

The Results of Technology in the Classroom

Technology use guidelines recommend no more than two hours of screen time daily for elementary and high school age students. With the amount of technology being used in education, children can easily end up spending several hours per day with digital devices overall. This much technology must demonstrate positive outcomes or the efforts to include technology in the classroom results in wasted money. Yet studies show technology can make it more difficult to learn and retain information. How does this play out in the classroom?[65]

Relying on Spell Check and AutoCorrect.
Studying how memories form, psychologists have discovered that coming up with a word in your own mind strengthens your memory. Autocorrect eliminates this memory-strengthening aspect of writing. This isn't the case when your device auto-corrects your spelling error or, even worse, offers "predictive text" options. People are losing the ability to spell on their own.

Relying on calculators.
While using calculators can help us save time, students can start to forget how to do simple operations such as multiplication and division! You can see this simple "use it or lose it" effect in math in your daily lives. Even as adults, the more you use calculators, the less you are able to remember the answer to 7x8.

Balance is the key. Banning helpful tools is not the goal, after all. Instead, education means ensuring that children can read, write, and do math, even when not supported by technological devices. Technology is at its most useful when it is thoughtfully added to the curriculum in a meaningful way. If it does not enhance the learning experience then it is a distraction.

Reliance on technology may be a contributing factor to a failing educational system. This is particularly true for the youngest learners. Too much technology at too young an age is not conducive to learning. Studies out of the University of Washington confirm that "educational" software geared towards babies and toddlers interferes with language acquisition and decreases vocabulary.[66]

It seems astonishing that the education system is not evidence-based in the sense that it's not referencing research. They are completely ignoring these guidelines. So many schools require over two hours of educational technology per day. They're completely discounting what pediatricians in North America advise and are moving forward with unrestricted use.

Alternative Education and Digital Schools

Excessive use of digital technology can occur when a child takes all classes online, or all subjects require digital media. Teaching children how to balance the activities they need to grow and succeed in school-based technology management programs is important. Parents need to consider alternative education and digital schools carefully. The facts support an implementation of school-wide technology management programs, but you need balance in order for children to grow and succeed, and to be ultimately successful with technology.

Kim's Corner
"Face-to-face instruction is always best. Online classes are a poor replacement for a live experience."

What is it about digital schools or online classes that make them inferior? Is it because of the lack of face-to-face experience with a teacher or is it something else? Or is it a combination of factors? Cris Rowan thinks one key issue is lack of supervision. She states:

> "I was listening to a CBS documentary and what they were saying was that many kids were just signing on in the morning and then they go and play video games all day. Then they log off in the late afternoon. They were getting little

supervision. It was taking two to three weeks for the online teachers to connect that this person wasn't producing any work. And then once they figured it out, the child was already into serious problems."

Supervision is necessary in combination with firewalls to filter online sites such as video games and porn sites. The parent of a child in an online school could have no idea what the child is doing online unless sitting right next to them.

Firewalls offer some protection, when the parent is not sitting alongside, but they are not a foolproof, teen-proof solution. These programs and applications can allow you to pre-approve websites your child can visit. However, teachers have inadvertently referenced inappropriate websites, sometimes porn, and a simple click from a lesson plan can steal a child's innocence in any unsuspecting family. Families with bright, well-rounded children can benefit from these courses, but you need to balance them carefully with parental supervision and involvement, to make sure your children gain quality educational value from the program, and don't fall off the tracks.

Avoid choosing online education due to social phobias. Leaning on technology can make matters worse. Choosing online school to withdraw your child from society avoids the problem, will not be a solution, and cannot be healthy. Your child may think, "I don't get along with kids. I don't have any friends, so I'm doing online learning." This avoidance can affect their future. If they can't connect with other kids now, when they're in school, they will have much less chance of forming meaningful relationships when they get older. Instead, you may want to provide the safety and security of interpersonal interaction through homeschooling your children, with the option of eliminating reliance on technology, and accentuating positive social interactions.

Carefully consider the age of your child before choosing education through technology. Age and maturity are important factors to consider, as suggested technology guidelines make clear. While some online learning may be appropriate for a teenager, it would be completely wrong for a six-year-old. Younger children need more movement, touch, connection, and nature. Older children need less. Children who are developmentally delayed or cognitively delayed also need more movement, touch, connection, and nature, and less "tech."

Cris' Counsel

"Digital schools and online classes are inferior because they lack the critical ingredients. Child development at every age involves physical movement, touch, interpersonal connection, and experience in nature."

Cris Rowan uses a balance beam metaphor to describe appropriate technology use. On one side of the balance beam are those four critical factors: movement, touch, connection, and nature. On the other side is technology. For young children, you want to load the balance beam so the four critical factors get much more emphasis. As your child gets older, it might level out so they get equal amounts. Consider your child's age, ability, and maturity. One hour of online class time balanced with one hour of face time might be appropriate for older children in middle school, or high school. But for elementary age children, this would still be too much technology. Children of all ages, but particularly elementary age children, need to go outside and be with people. They need to be hugged. They need interaction. The research strongly suggests they need to go out and play!

This should not be news to anyone. People are in danger of forgetting key truths that have long been considered common sense. Recess has always been a key part of elementary education. It is a critical part of children's overall development; it isn't only to get the kids out of the teacher's hair for a while. Studies show that children who move a lot are better able to pay attention and learn. They become measurably smarter. In John Ratey's book, *Spark*,[67] he profiles Naperville Florida High School, which improved test scores by adding physical movement, with the addition of an hour a day on treadmills. They observed huge differences, after only four months. This is more evidence that kids need exercise.

Online Classes and Homeschooling

Excessive hours of digital technology use can occur among homeschoolers as well. Homeschoolers may rely on many online classes and supplemental activities involving technology, sometimes exclusively. Kim McDaniel recommends that your child get one hour of face-to-face time for every hour of online class time. Try to find a balance of technology, print, and hands-on learning. If your child takes many technology-based classes, consider ensuring they read print books. Carefully restrict other technology use each day. Limiting non-educational digital media could provide balance.

Kim's Corner

"Online classes are a poor alternative to a live educational experience. Interpersonal interaction is essential to both learning and good mental health for children and teens. Of course, there are circumstances when they are necessary and valuable, such as an extended illness or a specialty course that is not otherwise available. The older the child, the better."

If you're a homeschooler, you need to be intentional about your children's friendships and other face-to-face interactions. You need to ensure there is adequate quality time with peers, with neighborhood friends, in co-ops, or in church groups. Adding exposure to digital technology through online classes may make the balance even harder to achieve.

Giftedness in Technology

Balancing technology becomes more complicated when children have special talents in computers, programming, and digital technology. These technologically gifted students can easily overuse digital technology and develop a serious problem. Their gifts and passions can lead to parents being permissive about screen time without restrictions. However, the developmental needs of gifted children are no different from regular kids. Even gifted children need movement, touch, connection, and nature. If you are the parent of a gifted child, you must conscientiously focus on the big picture, and development of your child as a whole person with a balanced life. Excessive screen time can sabotage career objectives, and discourage long-term success. A broad education will allow giftedness to come out in a variety of different ways, and ensures your child has the diversified education needed in order to achieve greater success.

You do not know how technology will be different when your children graduate from high school or college. You can't even be sure what technology will be like in the next three years. You know that it will get increasingly easier to use technology. Cris Rowan relates how one parent explained they provided technology to their two-year-old because they wanted them to understand technology. However, if you want your kid to grow up and drive a car, you don't teach them how to drive a car when they're two years old. It is developmentally inappropriate to give kids digital devices for this purpose. As Cris explains, digital devices rewire the child's brain and short-circuit the frontal lobe. Providing technology too early is almost ensuring your child will not do well in school, because they can't learn as well.

Technologic: How to Set Logical Technology Boundaries and Stop the Zombie Apocalypse

What do you want for your child? Most parents want them to be happy. Parents want children to be successful in whatever they do. This goal will be achieved through balance, and teaching children how to achieve balance with technology. The recipe for building such a child doesn't change with shifting technology. Children still need the same ingredients to be happy and healthy: movement, touch, connection, and nature.

Kim McDaniel has worked with many technologically gifted children. Her advice is to avoid a myopic, one-dimensional view, and to see the whole child. She gives pointed advice to parents with techie teens.

> "I have met with thousands of gifted children who express the desire to spend the majority of their lives working on a computer. The majority of their parents are so pleased with their career aspirations that they adopt a permissive attitude towards overuse of digital technology. I believe that a big picture perspective can be very helpful here.
>
> First, try to differentiate between a hobby and a professional aspiration. Then think about what marks a life well lived. There is a danger in allowing your child to channel their giftedness into a very specialized category when they are young. Such a child could miss learning new things about themselves, those qualities that often surprise us.
>
> Second, childhood and adolescence is the time for self-discovery and a certain amount of playfulness. It is through these experiences that we gain the skills and attributes that are necessary for us to succeed personally and professionally. There will always be time to hone the skills, do the training and prepare academically for a career in engineering. Extensive screen time may sabotage such career ambitions. I've met with too many gifted young people who find themselves unable to compete in the job market due to poor

interpersonal skills, anxiety, emotional inflexibility, and insecurities."

Gifted Children and Technology Abuse or Addiction

Are gifted children more prone to digital abuse and addiction? Perhaps, but it is more likely that gifted children are simply better at convincing parents that technology boundaries do not apply to them. It may be a little bit of both.

Cris Rowan has had a similar experience.

> "I have two children; they're grown up and both launched in careers. I grossly limited my son especially with technology, because I felt I was losing him. He was 12; he was getting surly and defiant, and spending hours down in his bedroom doing who knows what. I cancelled the cable. I threw out the TV, and the video games, and the computer. I had to replace what he was missing from these activities with something that was going to also help him to feel okay about himself. So I gave chores. I started with … 'You have to cook dinner every Friday night. You've got to do your laundry. These are two chores you need to do every week.' He got into the whole dinner thing, even inviting his friends over every Friday night and it turned into a big social thing that was happening over at our house. The funny thing was that the kids would come to our house because there wasn't technology. They would never say that to me, but they knew they could sit down at the dinner table and they were going to have a conversation. They were going to be listened to."

Cris continues:

> "My son and daughter are very similar, very accomplished. He's now back in school and working on his Masters in

Technologic: How to Set Logical Technology Boundaries and Stop the Zombie Apocalypse

---

Sustainable Research Development in Tidal Power. The choice to go 'no tech' with him I think was a good one, maybe a little radical, but it's not as scary as people think. Ask your child if they can bring you a piece of research that says technology is going to impact them in a meaningful, positive way when they graduate from high school. Look at the studies. Look at real, grounded research. Ask yourself if giving your child more technology when they are gifted is helping them become more social, and more self-regulated. Parents are going against the research by allowing unrestricted use of technology."

Kim's Corner

"Try to think about your child from a holistic perspective. Help him or her develop a balanced life, one that nurtures the soul. A gifted child needs just as much parental guidance as any other child, and they should not be allowed to set their own limits for digital technology."

Kim McDaniel is equally concerned about educating gifted children. Kim explains how parents can best care for their gifted children.

"If your child is gifted, don't make the mistake of letting him or her become a big fish in a little pond. In the real world he or she may be ill equipped to swim in the ocean with thousands of other big fish. Consider a study abroad program; expose your gifted child to different cultures, languages (other than computer languages) and divergent points of view. I have also worked with hundreds of engineers that come into counseling because they are unhappy."

Encouraging balance for childhood and the teen years, training children to limit technology, may help you avoid promoting unhappiness in the future. And as parents, you want your children to have a happy life in future, not only a happy hour playing video games in the present.

Ask yourself if your child is failing because they're not doing what they're supposed to, or whether they're failing because they're spending too much time on digital media. Failing school is often the first sign parents notice so it's something you want to stay on top of. Make sure you see your child's report cards throughout junior high and college. This can be more challenging when your child turns 18 and you are no longer legally entitled to their college records, even if you pay for college and all their bills. Arrange with your child that they must give you the password to view their online grades, or you will not pay for college. You may also want to turn your router off or take away technology at night to ensure they get much needed sleep.

Autism Spectrum Disorder and Technology Abuse or Addiction

Kim McDaniel says that children with autism spectrum disorders are more likely to have difficulty managing screen time. They are more vulnerable to developing problems with digital addiction. There are several reasons, with biological and psychological roots. From a child development perspective, any child who has difficulty with real life social interactions is more prone to turning to the computer to satisfy their social needs. The basis of empathy development, emotional resiliency, self-esteem, and overall good mental health comes from relationships with others. For those on the autism spectrum, their difficulty recognizing the undertones of language – subtle humor, sarcasm, contempt, flirting, and persuasion – also make them more vulnerable to bullying, peer pressure, and manipulation.

Cris' Counsel

"Autism is an attachment disorder, a child who cannot attach to other people, to their parents. Do we want to hand that child a device and detach them even further from humanity? That is the exact opposite of what we should be doing. Yet we're readily handing them iPads at the age of three or four. Delayed speech? Give him an iPad. We're further entrenching that child in a life of loneliness and detachment. If I was a parent of a child with autism, I would be using a lot of the more evidence-based research - interventions using play, using nature, using movement, all show promise for improving autism."

Research shows another side of the story. Overuse of technology can cause symptoms that mimic autism. Children can display the behaviors of someone with autism; they have been so disconnected from people they lose some of their social skills. Perhaps symptoms of autism may improve for some children when they increase social contact while at the same time decreasing technology use.

Even "educational" games can be strangely addictive. One of the most popular games right now is Minecraft. This seemingly harmless game gets a lot of positive attention due to its ability to promote creativity and imagination. But there is a darker side to it. Many parents whose children are deeply involved in Minecraft report that its addictive properties are unlike anything they have ever experienced. You will discover many such stories through a quick internet search on "Minecraft Addiction." Amazing, isn't it? Page after page of articles and columns with titles such as, "Help,

My Child is Addicted to Minecraft" and "How do I get my son to reduce his addiction to Minecraft?" Parents, tread carefully here. Even seemingly wholesome games can be detrimental to your children's development.

Minecraft is an extremely popular game. Parents are being pushed hard by their children to allow early usage of it. There are violent components to it and there are wonderful components, what Andy Doan, a colleague of Cris' terms "digital broccoli" and "digital candy." You have the positive part of Minecraft, the construction, the building … it's an amazing game and it could be pro-social. Sit down and play the game with your children, and see if you can work out some management tools steering them toward the more pro-social aspects of the game. Ask yourself, "Is my child social? Do they have friends? Do they go outside and play? Do they get along with their siblings? Do they sit down and eat dinner, and have a social conversation with the rest of the family? Is their development okay? Is their academic performance okay?" If for all of these questions, you're thinking, "check, check, check," then your child might be one who benefits from some aspects of Minecraft. If the reverse is the case, and your child is becoming asocial or antisocial (they don't want to go out anymore, they don't have any friends, they're grumpy all the time, angry, they're not wanting to come to the dinner table and socialize with the rest of the family, all they want to do is play video games) then you have a problem brewing.

Key Consideration in Education
Children need the maximum amount of face-to-face learning and physical activity. Education should use technological, digital, and online learning only as a supplement, not as a primary source of instruction. Technology in education is like adding salt to your food. Don't overdo it or you might end up with some serious health problems!

Prevent the Problem

CHAPTER 7

Ten Ways to Create Wholesome Technology Boundaries

You can help prevent the problems associated with technology without an absolute ban on devices (except for your very young children). Technology has become like the air you breathe. You can't escape it. You must learn how to deal with it. You have learned the many drawbacks of technology, but parents need solutions. What can you do about it? Children are children, with a limited understanding of right and wrong, unfamiliar with the long-term consequences of their behavior. You need to shape and mold your child's actions. You must look to your child's long-term health by setting technology boundaries.

1. Control Location
Start with the easiest way to limit technology. You can control the location of digital devices in your home. This is by far the easiest way of creating boundaries, and many major technology issues can be solved this way. This solution is easy to implement for all age groups, with clear and concise rules. Technology must be located in public areas only. Keep technology, such as digital devices, laptops, tablets, and PCs, in public areas of your home only, where they are visible to all. Make sure devices are never in the bedroom or bathroom. Technology should not be permitted at the dinner table. You can initiate a family rule that removes all devices at the dining table, to increase interaction between family members during meals.

Parent's Perspective

♡ "In our family, we have an agreement that my teen's tech gadgets must all go into a 'neutral zone' during school time, out of reach and out of earshot during the middle of the day."

~ A Homeschool Parent

Public locations limit intentionally inappropriate internet searches, because everyone knows the parent can easily check over the child's shoulder at any time. Teenagers are also less tempted to snap and share inappropriate photos online. Even preteens must understand technology location boundaries, to prevent a catastrophe of epic proportions. A Barrington, Illinois middle school provides ample warning of the failure to control locations.

Parent's Perspective

♡ "My 15 and 12-year-old boys must turn in all devices to a shelf in our den, the charging station, by 9:00 PM. No technology is allowed in the bedrooms at any time."

~Monica

A Barrington Police investigation of a sexting incident involved two middle school boys.[68] This was a criminal investigation and the outcome was extremely serious for the students involved. The police department urges parents to speak candidly with their children and ensure that cell phones and other technology remain in a neutral location in the house at night, not in the bedroom. Adults should understand the seriousness of a situation when the message comes from the police.

Technologic: How to Set Logical Technology Boundaries and Stop the Zombie Apocalypse

Begin teaching children rules about technology locations while they are young, to avoid problems with initiating new rules. Controlling the location is often the easiest starting place for even the most relaxed parent to begin setting boundaries.

2. Control Time
Limit the total amount of time spent with electronics each day. Follow the guidelines for technology set by the American Academy of Pediatrics. Set clear time limits, using a timer to monitor the hours. Give your child a limit, such as one or two hours of screen time per day, including all time spent in front of digital devices, even while watching siblings play or parents watch TV.

> ### Lee's Lessons
> "In my own home, we always used a timer to control media use. In the beginning, games were limited to 30 minutes each day. Later on, it was extended to an hour a day. My children are grown adults now, and they still love me, and were not harmed by careful monitoring."

Refer to the American Academy of Pediatrics and Canadian Pediatric Society guidelines, mentioned previously.[69] For age newborn to two, children should not use technology at all. For ages three to five, children can use technology for up to one hour a day, but no gaming or handheld devices at all. For ages six to twelve, children can spend up to two hours per day, but no handheld devices at all. For ages thirteen to eighteen, teenagers should have no more than two hours per day of personal technology use, and video games should be limited to 30 minutes per day, but no online violent games should be allowed.

Parent's Perspective

♡ "One of the best things that happened for us is that we asked our pediatrician in front of the kids what were good time limits. When they heard his answer, his authority helped us to maintain the boundaries we had at the time and as we move forward."

~ Kristin

Set a digital curfew at night. Turn off all digital devices at a set time each evening. Make sure your kids know there is no internet access after bedtime at all, from any device. You can set parental controls on video games and video game systems, which can shut off the games at a certain time each day, or between certain hours.

Parent's Perspective

♡ "We control the internet with parental locks through our internet router. We shut the internet off at 10:00pm until 6:00am through the router also. We take all the phones into our master bathroom each night and put them on silent. That way no sleep is interrupted."

~ Cindy

Remember that technology use and screen time includes TV viewing and watching screens used by parents or siblings. Television used to be a one-way medium, broadcast only, but technology has broken that boundary, allowing two-way communication. There's something about the internet and video games that make it a different ball game altogether.

Todd's Take

💡 "There are always people who come up to me after I speak and will say things like, 'people are going to be addicted to anything.' This is different. If you show me 10 people who are addicted to television, I'll show you 100 people who are addicted to video games."

3. Control Content

Control the content of digital media your children are exposed to. You probably didn't grow up with all this amazing technology, so it's critical to learn all you can about it so you can wisely protect your child. To control the content your child is exposed to, you need to purchase a current, up-to-date internet filter. Purchase an internet filter for every device.

Kim's Corner

"Every parent should monitor online behavior and use an internet filter. I recommend Net Nanny or McAfee Family Protection. We didn't have these options when my children were younger and I recommend them in the strongest possible terms."

Check the download and browsing history on every device regularly. The need for this may come as a surprise to parents who aren't aware of the scope of the problem. It's important to see what your children have been downloading and where they have gone online so you can start a conversation about anything inappropriate if necessary. You can get video tips online that clearly explain how to check your browser history, through commonsensemedia.org.

Parent's Perspective

Children may erase their search history. "We have told our kids that if the history is empty, we will assume they have been seeing things they shouldn't, and they won't be allowed to use computers for a period of time."

~Amy

Monitor your child's social media activity. For younger teens, you should possess all passwords, including all social media accounts. Look at all posts, direct messages, and photos shared. You can't protect against all the poor decisions that your children will make in the future, but you can still protect and guide them now, as they learn appropriate guidelines and boundaries for interacting online.

Todd's Take
Children can get around filtering devices. "One of my oldest sons said, 'I can get around all of them.' It's true, but I would still put those protections on even if they can get around them. Maybe from protecting them and talking to them, they will be less likely to want to go to those sites."

4. Teach Safety

Teach digital safety. Instruct your children not to share personal information online. Think about the most embarrassing moment of your life. How would you feel if a story or a photo of that moment popped up while you were at work giving a presentation, or if it was sent to all of your friends? This is what it's like for information floating around in cyberspace. It's not only out there, but it can also pop up at the least convenient time possible. Ensure your child never takes extremely personal photos or shares personal photos sent to them online or by cell phone. Remember, children who have forwarded compromising photos of other children have been charged with distributing child pornography. You must have these tough discussions with your children.

> ### Lee's Lessons
> "Think of each social media update, message, or post as if it were a digital tattoo that can never be removed."

Teach the permanence of posting online. This is a difficult concept for most children to understand. Think of each social media update, message, or post as if it were a digital tattoo that can never be removed. A post may seem cool to them now, but how will your child feel if that photo is floating out there when they're 30, 40, or 50 years old? How would they feel if their parent or grandparent posted it?

Teach your child about privacy and internet safety regularly. Common Sense Media (commonsense.org) shares the following safety tips to teach young children.[70]

- Children should never share their name, school, age, phone number, address, or even show photos with this information online.
- They should never send pictures to strangers.
- Teach them to keep passwords private except to you as parents.
- They should never open emails from strangers because they could contain viruses.
- Have them immediately tell an adult if something mean or creepy happens.
- Allow them to visit only age-appropriate sites.
- Have them do internet searches with you as parents.
- Make sure they avoid strangers.
- Tell your child that people aren't always who they say they are when they're in cyberspace.

- Teach your child to be a good cyber citizen, and play nice. A good rule of thumb is, if they wouldn't do it in real life, then don't do it online.
- Cheating is always a no-no, pure and simple, whether they're online or in real life.
- Keep the computer in a central location so everybody can see what's going on.
- Establish clear boundaries.

Common Sense Media (commonsense.org) also has the following safety tips for older children and teens.

- Give your teens a code of conduct.
- Tell them that if they wouldn't say something to a person's face, they shouldn't say it online either.
- Remind your teenagers to use social network privacy settings so only friends can see what they post.
- Tell them not to share photos with strangers.
- Have them keep everything private.
- Teach your child to be a good digital citizen and flag inappropriate content. If they see something that shouldn't be online, they need to tell someone, notify the webmaster, etc.
- The golden rule applies in cyberspace, if they wouldn't do it in real life, they shouldn't do it online.
- Parents of teens should always agree on every download, and what is okay as far as music, videos, and games.
- Encourage critical thinking so your child can ask, "Who posted this and why?" And then they can even ask themselves, "Why am I posting this? Who will see it? Could it be misunderstood?"

Each safety rule and suggestion has a reason behind it, and a potential conversation you can have with your children. In the digital age, you must step up and provide digital safety to cover a variety of settings and scenarios.

> *Parent's Perspective*
>
> ♡ "Amen to all of this. I've had to experience all of the negatives, because I was too naive for my own good. There's good in being naive, and then there is stupidity, especially when it comes to protecting your children from porn. Please do heed the warnings here. If I had only known, I would have been more responsible about parenting in this area. I am very sad for my son who was exposed to this for years."
>
> ~Renee

5. Exchange Activities

Exchange digital devices for low-tech fun, and replace screen time with fun activities. These activities might include reading, projects, family games, evenings out, day trips, holding an entire unplugged celebration night, or taking a walk with your dog. Brainstorm some non-tech activities that your family enjoys, or used to enjoy, before the latest gadgets. Children need to understand what it's like to have fun without screens or the internet. Create an unplugged evening filled with games, activities, and face-to-face social time.

> *Parent's Perspective*
>
> ♡ "We have family game night several times a week, and have fun together with board games."
>
> ~ Kristin

Pets are a great exchange. Many pets make great therapy animals. If your child is having problems unplugging, they don't enjoy anything, or are experiencing sadness or depression, dogs are great therapy animals. Pets provide unconditional love that can be helpful to people experiencing depression or distress. The uncomplicated, unconditional love of a dog can increase activity, fitness, companionship, social interaction, and touch. Studies have shown that people who have pets are healthier overall than people who do not.[71] If you have trouble separating your children from technology, pets make an especially good replacement.

6. Model Behavior
Kids learn best by example, and a good leader will show the way. You as parents need to demonstrate appropriate self-control over your own technology use. Demonstrate your commitment to digital etiquette in your own behavior. Show children that there are times for appropriate use of technology, but also times when it's important to be free of digital media. Have them shut down the devices when hosting visitors, visiting with friends or family, mealtime, dining at a restaurant, various outings, dates, and group activities.

Parent's Perspective
"I had my phone off the other day in the morning while we were schooling because I noticed how distracting it was getting. When I turned it on at lunch break, I had 14 messages! The kids were surprised, but it sure helps them respect boundaries when my husband and I keep those boundaries - and they SEE us keep those boundaries."

~ Homeschool Mom

Technologic: How to Set Logical Technology Boundaries and Stop the Zombie Apocalypse

A pediatrician noticed that more and more parents were coming into his office with their digital devices. In the article, "Parenting While Distracted,"[72] Dr. Jane Scott wrote about a father who brought in his two-year-old son to the medical clinic. The father and son sat next to each other, but did not look at each other or talk to each other. Completely silent, both scrolled and tapped through their digital devices. The doctor gave the toddler an exam and the father directed most of her questions to the toddler, who said that his ear hurt. Discovering his eardrums were red and inflamed, the doctor said, "You have an ear infection." This little two-year-old child turned to his iPad, pushed the button and said, "Siri, what's an ear infection?" With a shocking lack of parent-child interaction, instead of asking his father, the two-year-old asked a computer.

Lee's Lessons

"I had dinner with a close friend, and she kept two cell phones on the table the entire time we were together. She took five to ten phone calls, texting in between, as we shared a meal. At one point, she put one cell phone on hold, to take a call from the other cell phone. We had little time to exchange information, much less share feelings, friend to friend. It felt uncomfortable. I didn't want to meet her for dinner anymore, even though we used to get together every two months."

You may see similar behaviors all around you, in various social circles. "Do as I say, not as I do," has never been a good approach to parenting. They will do what you do, especially when you're dealing with something as insistent and pervasive as digital media.

7. Hold a Family Meeting

Discuss technology use as a family and teach personal safety during a family meeting. Use news reports to share current learning opportunities. Share news stories about cyber-bullying, pornography, or sexting with your children, in an age-appropriate manner. Inform your children that you will check their cell phones, social media, and internet history. Give teens a code of conduct. Tell your children that they should never post something online they wouldn't say to a person's face. Remind children that you will check up on them. Explain to children that it is a parent's job to check phones, social media accounts, and internet surfing history to ensure the safety of the entire family. Take the job seriously and set rules in place, before serious trouble occurs. If difficulty arises, the tradition of holding a family meeting will provide a safe place to talk about what happened, why, and how to avoid it in the future.

Kim McDaniel adds that a family meeting should include creating a technology contract, as an exercise the whole family participates in. The parents establish the primary boundaries and the children provide some input. During this meeting, a daughter may express embarrassment by her mother's talking on the phone during her gymnastics lessons, for example. List the house rules of when, where, and how much technology, as non-negotiable rules established by the parents. Then list some new, non-tech, activities that you can do together. Conclude the discussion with the creation of a written document, on a whiteboard, chalkboard, or paper, and have all family members sign their names in agreement. Then display the contract in a prominent location as your family technology contract for all members to follow.

Parent's Perspective

"Grandparents need to be educated, too. The only time my daughter saw anything inappropriate online was when she was eight years old and her grandparents let her get on the computer and Google something Christian-related. But my daughter mistyped and up popped the porn. She ran off and told her grandparents, but they had no idea what was going on. We never allow her to get on and search for anything, but we had forgotten to inform the grandparents who were watching her."

~ Camille

8. Teach Discernment

Kim also believes that families need to teach discernment at a young age. Explain what is appropriate for each device. Reinforce the family rules as they apply to technology. Discuss the consequences of behavior online, such as the permanence of online posts, and personal safety issues. Talk about the possibility of digital addiction, and the future consequences of long-term behavior. Reinforce family rules and extend those into digital rules: no inappropriate language, no posting anything mean about anyone, and no harassing or insulting comments about others, even when teens think the comments are private.

Parent's Perspective

"My daughter was asked for (explicit) pictures. She told us right away, and her brother spoke to the boy and told him not to contact her again. That was a year ago. She is 13."

~ Cindy

Keep discussion age-appropriate. Talk about keeping private parts private. Explain that private areas are usually covered by a swimsuit. For younger children, use this swimsuit definition to explain privacy or sexting in a language they can understand. For older children, make sure you teach that the internet is forever and that nothing is ever truly deleted or private. It seems as if every day in the news, you see somebody has embarrassing pictures hacked or leaked somehow to the press. Look at the latest news report and speak to your teenager about it. They probably know about it anyway, so use it as an example of how nothing is private. Online behavior is permanent.

9. Establish Expectations
Set clear boundaries on technology use. Follow with clear cause-and-effect consequences for violating family rules. Breaking rules demonstrates that teens are not able to moderate their own behavior, and they need help. You can help your child maintain technology boundaries by removing the device causing difficulty until they are able to control technology in their life again.

Consistently following the rules indicates that a teenager is able to control their own behavior and can handle additional trust. Clear expectations and consequences are almost magical in their power to influence teen behavior. Parents should have a conversation together before laying down the consequences, so you agree, and the children know exactly what is expected and the outcome if rules are disobeyed. Once you establish expectations, it is critical that you follow through.

Parent's Perspective
♡ "Any type of technology is considered a privilege and not a right in our home. We use a system of the amount of minutes you exercise, clean, and read, which collectively equals the minutes earned for technology use."
~Lorrie

Technologic: How to Set Logical Technology Boundaries and Stop the Zombie Apocalypse

If your child won't comply with your technology rules, then they don't get access to technology in your home. For the first offense, they could lose their technology privileges for a week. For their second offense, they could lose their technology privileges indefinitely or until they are proven trustworthy. You may have them use a basic mobile phone instead of a smartphone, without any texting capabilities or internet access. Perhaps they even have to do their research at the library using books. Be cautious of unmonitored internet access at the library, though.

Lee's Lessons

"There was controversy in my town about viewing pornography on library computers and ultimately the library decided it was a free speech issue. Children, teens, and adults can access porn in the public library even where it's visible to children. The screens don't even have privacy filters, so what people are viewing can easily be seen simply walking by a computer. In the library with my children when they were in middle school, I saw pornography on a library computer as we walked past to check out some books."

Kim McDaniel suggests that parents set the expectation that a child does not have privacy. You pay the phone bill, and the phone belongs to you. You pay for the internet connection, and your child has the privilege of using it only when allowed. Let children know in advance that you will be checking their emails, photos, messages, and contacts. Have a serious discussion about online predators, cyber bullying, and sexting.

10. Create Balance

Technology is part of daily life. You need it to function in your daily, modern life. Children and teens should not be prevented from using technology completely. You should not limit it so much that your child becomes fearful, incapable, or unprepared. At the same time, it must be restricted enough so your child is able to develop life skills, not only technology skills.

Schools should create a balanced educational plan. They must teach some online or technical skills, such as keyboarding, internet, email, technology, and coding. At the same time, they should balance online education with non-digital, non-electronic coursework.

> ### Lee's Lessons
> "Homeschoolers must create a balanced educational plan that includes technology for difficult subjects and technical computer skills. Go technology-free and low-tech for coursework when possible. This balanced plan must not exceed the recommendations from the American Academy of Pediatrics. Home education can be a challenge, but limit technology to a total of two hours a day, including both educational and recreational time."

Seek a balance between fun involving technology and recreation that does not involve technology of any kind. Balance and moderation are key for parents in general. Never is this more the case than with teenagers and technology. If you overstate your case, you invite rebellion. Ignoring it completely risks damage to your child's character and future.

Technologic: How to Set Logical Technology Boundaries and Stop the Zombie Apocalypse

Parenting is tough. Parenting teenagers is even tougher. Parenting during the technology age is tougher still.

While not a panacea for technology abuse, time spent in active play with a parent can help. Activity keeps your child focused, occupied, and a little exhausted. It demonstrates a real and tangible way they are loved, and it enables them to avoid many of the troubles that face families today.

CHAPTER 8

Nine Real Family Examples of Setting Successful Technology Boundaries

Steve Jobs, one of the founders of Apple, created many of the techie devices in use today. You might expect that his home was filled with technology. Surprisingly, Steve Jobs was a "low-tech" parent.[73] In the technology industry, many chief executives and venture capitalists are similarly low-tech. Shockingly, adults in the technology business are much more likely to be low-tech parents than other adults are. Presumably, they want to avoid the dangers of technology, such as exposure to pornography, cyber bullying, and addiction.

Many have strict rules limiting their children's time with digital devices. Rules may include no devices on school nights and strict time limits on weekends. Their homes are filled with real, physical, unplugged books and toys. Their children have hundreds of physical books lining their shelves to read. For many, their children aren't allowed to use smartphones until age 14 and don't get their own until age 16. Every evening, Steve Jobs' family sat together for supper at the kitchen table. All of these techie parents have one rule in common, not one of them allowed screens in bedrooms.

Your goal is to control the content your children are exposed to, and the time they spend with technology. Your goal is also to teach and model safety, spend more time together as a family, and create a good balance in your family life.

What may technology boundaries look like for a typical family? Here are some real family examples of successful technology boundaries at home. These ideas are parent-tested and work.

1. Meal Time
For many families, the simplest, easiest, and most concrete way to set boundaries is to limit technology at the dining table. Dawn says, "Meals are for food and family, not technology. Our rule is 'no toys at the table' and that includes tech gadgets and books." Pam has a system to make sure the rule is followed, "We put all phones and handheld devices in a basket during dinner time. Nobody is allowed to take their device out until Dad says the mealtime is over."

2. Bed Time
It's critical to keep all technology out of the bedroom. This boundary is important to ensure quality sleep and limit the risk of inappropriate and often unanticipated behavior, such as sending personal information to others, or viewing personal information on inappropriate websites. Pamela has a simple solution for her home, "All technology is brought to a designated place at bedtime. When the children forget, or if I remind them, they lose the privilege for using that device the following day."

> *Parent's Perspective*
> "We allow screen time from 6:00pm to 8:00pm. This makes sure they've done their school and chores, and screens are turned off in time to wind down for sleep."
> ~ Robin

Technologic: How to Set Logical Technology Boundaries and Stop the Zombie Apocalypse

3. Friend Time
Technology interferes with true socialization, and the development of long-term friendships and positive relationships. Real friendship develops offline. It's important to keep non-wired life fun, and keep social skills sharp and the only way to do that is to be with friends in real life, not in a digital life. Drea says that she monitors friend time at her home, "No technology when friends are over unless it's specifically a planned 'gaming' time."

4. Common Area
Keeping all technology in a common area can limit inappropriate surfing, and reduce feelings of guilt if they are surprised by vulgar content popping up in the presence of parents, who witness that it was through innocent behavior. Jina keeps her household rule simple, "Computer time is limited to the common area, where everyone in the family can easily see the screen. Parent screen time is only used when children are not around."

5. Family Time
Deb makes sure her children play online games in a social setting, to avoid having them over-use technology in an isolated way. She says, "Nobody plays video games unless we all play video games together." How much time could you spend online if everyone in the family, even parents, agreed to play at the same time? An hour or two? Eventually someone would want dinner, and when one person quits, everyone quits.

Lee's Lessons
"My husband and I were at a convention, and the booth next to us was a young Christian family with a small business. They were there with their two young children, about age one and three. While it

was nice to see them together as a family all day, these two very young children were in a playpen with digital devices for the entire weekend-long convention. During those long convention days, for about 12 hours straight each day, we watched these babies in a playpen with digital devices, receiving little human interaction. Ironically, their business was focused on building character in young children."

6. Focused Attention
Many parents have a rule to keep focused attention on real people, not on technology. One parent requires undistracted attention, "When anyone is spoken to, their personal technology must be turned over, closed, or turned off, giving the speaker their undivided attention." Another mom shares, "We don't allow technology in cars, because that is where family can come together and can share with each other, uninterrupted." Instead of isolating themselves with personal devices, they created family time during their commute.

7. No Isolation
Isolation, and becoming engrossed in technology, is often the beginning of big trouble. Melody works to prevent isolation in her home, "Digital isolation is not allowed. Children can't play video games alone, and when they do play, they are limited to one hour. Video games are allowed only if it is raining outside, and the child is done with all other chores or school work."

8. Only Weekends
Limiting technology to certain days can make it easier for children to understand. Some parents may allow technology only a few days

Technologic: How to Set Logical Technology Boundaries and Stop the Zombie Apocalypse

each week. Laura says, "Gaming and videos are allowed only on weekends when we do not have outings. This usually amounts to two evenings a weekend at most. Otherwise, allow no TV or technology, because children have a lot of living to do!"

9. Before Bedtime
Sleep is important for both adults and children to function. A big parenting priority is to keep all technology away from sleeping areas. It may seem inconvenient, but it's extremely important for your child's growth and development. Technology-free time is important for adults, too, because even parents need quality sleep. Pam says, "In our family, we turn off all media at 9:00pm, so our brains have time to calm down and our spirits have time for quiet reflection before bed."

Setting clear, consistent boundaries is critical for families. The easier the rule is to understand, the more likely your family can maintain the rule. It may seem inconvenient to set boundaries, but it is extremely important for your child's growth and development.

Lee's Lessons

"When one of my sons was young, he needed nebulizer treatments for asthma multiple times a day. The only way I could get the little guy to sit still was by showing him videos. He watched about 10 minutes of Sesame Street, four times a day, while he took his medication. To limit his exposure to technology, I was careful never to let him sit in front of a screen at any other time of day. We didn't watch TV or videos in our house until the children were in bed, and weren't watching with us."

CHAPTER 9

Seven Steps for Safe and Sane Internet Use

Only you can prevent the real zombie apocalypse in your home! Here are some steps for creating technology boundaries to help your children thrive.

1. Step up and be the parent
Your job is your priority. You are in charge of setting technology boundaries. Your job when your child is young is not to be their friend; your job is to be their parent. Shape and mold your child's character. It gets harder as they get older. Do your best to have the maximum influence on your child when they're young. Keep your child involved in real life. Hold family meetings, talk to them often, and discuss the stories you see on the news. Get your child involved in sports, music, and art activities so they are used to engaging in activities that do not involve technology. As your child gets older, recognize that you cannot control another adult. Your adult child has to make their own choices. You are only responsible for your own behavior, not your grown child's behavior.

2. Lead by example
Demonstrate responsible behavior with your own internet usage, whether online, playing games, on your phone, or using social media. If your child struggles with abuse or addiction to the

internet, you are never online, and never use digital devices in your child's presence. Avoid using the phone, other than to place an important call. Demonstrate behavior that places people above technology. Be an example of wise technology management. At the same time, be transparent about your struggles. This will give your children permission to share their own struggles with you. This is not a time to be stoic. Kicking an internet habit is hard work. Going through it together as a family will make it easier for everyone.

Todd's Take
"The best way to teach our children this concept is by doing it ourselves. I can't tell you how many wives have written me saying, 'We call our husband's telephone his mistress because he always has to answer.' I had a mom who wrote me not too long ago who said they were having an intimate time when the phone buzzed. He rolled over to answer! She was devastated because his phone was more important than her. We've been trained to think that we have to respond immediately. The truth is, we don't! You can wait until the morning to respond to an email. I think it begins with us as parents. This is not just a kid thing. This is a mom and dad thing."

3. Keep technology in a public area
Keeping technology in a public area enables you to avoid inappropriate behaviors and assess potential problems. It doesn't matter how many commercials your child sees of teenagers using their cell phones and laptops in their bedrooms; don't give in. Technology

should always be in a public place to avoid inappropriate behavior, limit temptation, and allow you to assess potential problems as your child grows older.

Lee's Lessons

"The buyers of our last home were appalled that we didn't have cable outlets in every bedroom. They didn't know how it was possible to have a child's room without a TV, but my own children never had TVs in their bedrooms."

4. Install filters and monitoring software

Research and install devices meant to filter online content. Ensure these helpful resources are always up to date. Don't make the mistake of assuming they solve the total problem, however. These devices alone cannot keep your child safe, but they're tools that can help. They are only tools in your arsenal; they can't eliminate problems alone.

Cris' Counsel

"Advertisers and pornographers are becoming more and more clever in where they bury their hidden messages, and so I consider internet filter tools as essential as having anti-virus software."

5. Turn the internet off at night

Each evening, completely remove the ability for a child to use online resources at night. This may be as simple as collecting devices every night. In more challenging situations, it may mean turning off online access for the whole house. This technique will prevent your child from cheating house rules, or sneaking around to use the internet. This is important, because nighttime use can create sleep interruptions that can spiral out of control.

6. Set up internet-free times
Teach your family how to have fun without digital devices of any kind. Spend time engaging in wholesome technology-free activities to provide alternatives your child enjoys. Providing internet-free times will help your family remember the parts of real life that can be fun. Would you let your child sit in a movie theater or in front of a TV for eight hours at a time? Probably not. Yet parents may allow children to hold their phones and to text and engage in social media for many hours at a time. A screen is a screen. See it for what it is. Don't let your child sit in front of a digital device for that long.

> *Lee's Lessons*
> "I love the idea of 'sacred time' as Cris suggests. It demonstrates that your child is your priority."

7. More technology is not the solution to your technology problem
The problems of technology can't be solved with more technology. If you purchase technology to solve your problem, you will be disappointed – it can only provide a false sense of security. The ultimate answer to technology is not more technology, but less. The best answer is your parental love and involvement, and providing real life experiences rather than only digital fun. If you give a man a fish, he can eat for a day; but if you teach a man to fish, he can eat for a lifetime. With technology, if you teach your child to set boundaries, they can establish boundaries for a lifetime.

Deal With The Problem

CHAPTER 10

How to Successfully Unplug: Dealing with Troublesome Technology

In the digital age, parenting is becoming more difficult. The desire to start unplugging children is becoming an increasingly common theme. Parents need tools to help them unplug across a variety of formats, from TV and video games, to the internet and handheld devices. Because unplugging is so important, you want to spend some conscious effort thinking about how you can do this the right way. You want your family to unplug successfully from excess and live to tell about it.

How important is reducing technology? It's as important as providing your child with well-balanced meals, clean clothes, and a quality education. It is as important as providing for the safety and welfare of your child, and protecting them from predators. You want to develop a plan for how to unplug your child without losing your cool or going down an unhealthy path yourself. This must be a priority in your home, to provide for your child's mental, physical, and emotional health.

Lee Binz, The HomeScholar

> *Parent's Perspective*
> ♡ "My 17-year-old son has wasted the last few years of school on excessive gaming/online time. How can I wean him off this? My husband sees no harm but my son is beginning counseling in August. It is so sad to see a bright, capable, young man waste these precious years."

The American Academy of Pediatrics recommends no more than two hours of technology use per day, yet one study claims that elementary children average eight hours per day.[74] Cris Rowan recommends ten healthy ways to unplug your child.

Ten Steps to Unplug Your Child[75]

1. Become Informed

You've already taken the first step to becoming informed by reading this book. Continue to learn about the effects of technology on physical and mental health. The American Academy of Pediatrics recommends only two hours of internet use per day, including all TV, video games, and digital devices. Overuse of technology is linked to:

- weight gain
- attention problems
- poor school performance
- poor body image
- trouble sleeping
- family conflict
- developmental delays
- attachment disorders
- addiction

- aggression
- early sexual experiences

The signs of technology addiction include:

- tolerance
- withdrawal
- unintended use
- persistent desire
- excessive time spent
- displacement of other activities
- continued use

2. Disconnect Yourself

As they recommend during pre-flight instructions, "Put on your own oxygen mask first and then put one on your child." The airlines know that a parent can't help their child unless they care for their own needs first. If you don't take care of yourself first, you could lose consciousness and your child would not survive. It's similar with technology. If you are deeply involved in technology, you may effectively lose consciousness, ignoring the needs of your family. Take care of your own internet issues first, then you can help your child disconnect.

Disconnect yourself; be available and present for your child. This may be the most challenging step. It is far easier to tell your child how to behave than to implement the changes for yourself. In the process of disconnecting yourself, you will become more available to your child, which is so important for developing connections that will result in a well-rounded, functional young person. Your child will model your behavior, so disconnecting yourself first also makes you a good role model. It will help to let them hear about your struggles as well. This will build credibility so they don't think you are unwilling to do what you ask of them. Model balancing technology use with other activities.

3. Reconnect with Family
Prioritize parent-child attachment. A healthy attachment lasts until your child is 18 years old and beyond. You want to connect with your child and give bear hugs to reconnect with them, even as they grow into adulthood. Many parents choose to be stay-at-home parents so they can always be available to their child. But if you've made that commitment to stay at home with your child but you're on your phone all the time, then you're not available to them. You have to take advantage when they're ready to talk, especially with teenagers, who might not always share their feelings freely. Being available for your child is important no matter what their age.

> **Cris' Counsel**
> "You need to create a time, I call it sacred time, where you're available to those kids and they know you're available, and you do not pick up the device during that time. Designation of 'sacred time' in the day with no technology (during meals, in the car, before bedtime, and holidays) is a first start toward reconnecting with your children."

Make time each day for only you and your child. Turn off your devices or put them in another room. Play board games or play outside together. If you can, set aside a specific time each day to unplug together.

4. Explore Alternatives
Find alternatives to technology to enjoy as a family. Not all children are interested in or value the same activities as adults. Find activities your child enjoys. They can ride a bike, climb a tree, create art,

Technologic: How to Set Logical Technology Boundaries and Stop the Zombie Apocalypse

wrestle, build a fort, dance, listen to music, cook, play cards, play a board game, garden, read a book, play a sport, or bake cookies. Listen to what they want. Foster a tolerance for individual differences. Respecting individual preferences can go a long way toward promoting a child's motivation to unplug.

Lee's Lessons

"I used to say to my kids, 'If you're bored then you must be boring.' There are always non-tech alternatives when kids say, 'I'm bored.' Sometimes it feels like children only find boredom-busters that involve more technology, not less. But more technology is not the solution."

When parents initially remove excess technology, children may respond by expressing boredom. Cris Rowan explains the complexity of the problem.

> "Children who only know video games or only know TV don't have a repertoire in their brain of other things to do. So you can't say, 'Go do something else. Put down the tech and go do something else.'"

As parents, you have to take responsibility for the state of your child. After all, technology may be all they have been practicing! Help them to identify alternative interests and work to explore them together.

Todd's Take

"When my little kids come into our bedroom first thing in the morning, oftentimes one will say, 'Hey Dad or Mom, can I look at pictures on your phone?' He wants to go through the photo album, and there's nothing bad on there, so it's no big deal. But I will always say, 'No, you can't.' And my wife will ask, 'Why not?' The reason is I don't want to train him that he has to fill up all his spare time by doing something on a phone."

Start observing your child. They will likely need help identifying their interests. When you ask, "What are you interested in doing?" your child may say, "nothing" or "everything's boring but video games" or "all I want to do is video games." It's not your job to find something else for your child to do, but it is your job to help them explore alternative interests, and perhaps create a list for the fridge or a schedule. Include indoor and outdoor activities, activities they can do alone, with their siblings and friends, and activities you can do as a family. You can create the list during a family meeting. Your job is to make sure what your child needs is available.

Cris' Counsel
"I always kept a deck of cards on my dining room table, and that was our default activity. We played a game of cards because it was always there and we always had one in the car as well. It gave us something to do other than the technology."

5. Enhance Performance Skills
Children with technology addictions have poorly developed identities, social skills, and relationships with nature. Cris Rowan explains that it is important to enhance these performance skills prior to unplugging your children.

Technologic: How to Set Logical Technology Boundaries and Stop the Zombie Apocalypse

"Drastically or suddenly reducing technology with a child who has an addiction will result in chaos at school and home, as the child is now alienated from what has become their whole meaning for living. Teachers and parents can help build performance skills by exposing children to activities that are not too hard, and not too easy. The child must be capable of being successful, rather than face constant failure in non-tech activities.

What you choose depends on the level of severity of the addiction. If your child has a severe addiction, then you may need a more severe strategy, a 'digital detox' if you will. This might be done in a facility or with the experience of a trained counselor, usually an addiction counselor. When we talk about going cold turkey, recognize there are a lot of ramifications of that. It may be justified in a severe situation, but recognize that it would require a lot of preparation and assistance from other professionals."

Cris continues:

"In the better case scenario, we don't have severe symptoms. We just have a child who's overusing and we need to start cutting down. There is a potential for addiction and we are trying to stop that from progressing. In those cases, you need to do some planning. Have a family meeting, like a team meeting. Your message should be about what you have learned about technology overuse and we want to start cutting down. But before we're going to cut down, we want to explore and establish our alternate skills and build some performance levels in those skills.

Often the parents will just say, 'Why don't you just play soccer? Why don't you just go shoot some hoops?' This can be trouble if the child has no motor skills and they've never done activity like that before. It can lead to performance anxiety in the child because they may be great at video games and just suck at everything else. They're not going to go out there and do something they're terrible at, and have everyone look at them and judge them. So it really is the parent's responsibility to begin helping the child build a performance level they can start to feel some confidence about. It is critical in order for them to be full participants in their return to health and a balanced life."

Cris' Counsel
"One child agreed to unplug. We needed to do a digital detox and he started saying, 'I'm only good at video games.' When we started talking about the alternate activities and building skills, his perception of his own skill level was so low he cried and said, 'But I'm not good at anything else.'"

6. Meet Developmental Milestones
Help your child meet developmental milestones through engagement in the three critical factors for child development: movement, touch, and connection.

Lee's Lessons
"My husband and children were constantly rough and tumble. Even through the high school years, they were often playing basketball, having squirt-gun fights, and roughhousing in the neighborhood pool. At the time, I nagged them to be careful. Now I find out these activities were great for development."

Technologic: How to Set Logical Technology Boundaries and Stop the Zombie Apocalypse

---

Cris Rowan explains the benefits of rough and tumble play.

> "Children need rough and tumble play three to four hours per day, while spending time connecting with their parent, teacher, and other children, in order to achieve optimal physical and mental health. This type of play promotes proper sensory development of the vestibular, proprioceptive, tactile, and attachment systems, which are all necessary for paying attention, printing, and reading."

Self-perception of skills and abilities is critical. As the child gains confidence and skill, through more movement, touch, connection, and accessing nature, they will feel they can step into the world with more confidence and understanding of their abilities.

Cris continues:

> "It doesn't have to be sports or even physical activity. Some children, who have been sedentary much of their lives, may feel much less threatened by a more sedate hobby, such as stamp collecting. That is a perfectly acceptable way for them to start building some performance level and confidence. If they can do that with an interested mentor or relative, you can then be both building skill and building connection. Be excited that they have identified an interest, even if it is nothing you would ever pursue yourself. The key is getting away from the tech while doing something they enjoy and can begin to excel in. Exercise and nature are still important for such children, but it can be in a much more relaxed fashion, without the performance pressure of organized sports."

7. Address Perceptions of Safety

Society's twenty-four hour news cycle has created a perception that the world is an unsafe and hazardous place. As you see reports of missing children, faulty playground equipment, and injured crime victims, it's easy to think your world is less safe than it used to be. Children are kept inside the house which parents perceive as safer, but where children watch more TV, play more video games, and spend time with technology.

Lee's Lessons

"During my own childhood, our entire neighborhood stayed out until well after dark to play kick the can across many blocks. My cousin's mother used to say, 'You can go out on your bike but stay on the south side,' which was approximately a 10-mile radius."

The perception of safety has changed so dramatically, but in reality, the world is much safer than it used to be. Many of today's parents perceive outdoor play is unsafe, even though the overwhelming majority of crimes against children are instigated by family members.

You have two jobs when raising your child, create a secure base and then launch your child into the world. In this culture, failure to launch is a growing concern. Media has propagated the perception that the world is a dangerous, evil place. It implies that pedophiles are on every corner, waiting to abduct your children. It suggests that even nature can't be trusted. As parents become more fearful of society and nature, they gravitate to technology.

Parents are afraid to let their older teens engage in normal activities, such as riding the bus, merely out of fear. Yet these same, overly careful parents may not even have basic computer firewalls protecting their children online. While they overstate the threats

Technologic: How to Set Logical Technology Boundaries and Stop the Zombie Apocalypse

of the real world, they understate the threats in the online world. The most popular online sites are used by real pedophiles to attract children into abduction, pornography and prostitution. Human trafficking has skyrocketed and they use gaming and social media sites to lure young people away from their homes. Being online is not necessarily safe.

> **Lee's Lessons**
> "Parents tend to use and allow more technology because they perceive it to be safer than society or nature, but it's not."

It is important for parents to talk to each other about their own perceptions of safety, when children aren't listening. Single parents should ask a friend, "Am I too safe with my child? Am I not safe enough?" Seek input from others about your perceptions of safety, and then consider whether you need to modify your parenting approach. You want to keep your child safe, but must focus on skill building as they get older. Your child must develop the skills needed in the real world, so they become street-wise, and savvy in the ways of the world. Make sure they are knowledgeable and have the basic life skills they need.

Cris Rowan explains that exposure to green space, and nature in general, results in a significant reduction in ADHD symptoms, in both areas of impulse control and attention ability. Children have a biological need for rough and tumble play, and it has been proven to reduce ADHD significantly. Time spent in nature not only has attention restorative benefits, but also activates all the senses to enhance multi-sensory learning ability.[76] Studies have shown that access to "green space" for 20 minutes per day significantly reduces ADHD symptoms. Inner city children suffer from ADHD at three times the rate of children in rural areas.[77]

Participation in physical activity is positively related to children's academic performance.

> ### Cris' Counsel
> "Roughhousing is amazing, and especially for dads and sons. For moms, it's a little harder, and girls tend to not like it as much. But it is great for those critical factors, vestibular, proprioceptive, tactile, and attachment. It's all there with roughhousing."

8. Foster Independence

Create individual roles, and foster independence in your children. Help them become confident and capable by assigning household chores. You're not being a mean parent or assigning chores for your own benefit, but because it's important for them. Help your child become a confident adult, by helping them learn life and career skills. Developing their ability to get a job outside the home at a young age can also be helpful.

Society perceives children as being grown-up when they're 18, 20, or 25 years old. In previous generations, however, children were perceived as being adults at a much younger age. Cris Rowan explains that parents can foster independence:

> "Realistic challenges and expectations from parents and teachers promote defined roles for children, and provide a structure where they can begin to try out new skills. When faced with a task that is perceived to be beyond a child's skill level, frustration and poor self-esteem can often be the result."

Technologic: How to Set Logical Technology Boundaries and Stop the Zombie Apocalypse

Fifty years ago, almost all children had real, meaningful work. In fact, they not only had jobs but if they didn't do their jobs, their families could perish. For example, in a family farm, someone had to milk the cows, feed the horses, chop the wood, and make the bread. Children had well-defined roles, with jobs that were meaningful and needed to be done. They gained a sense of importance from these jobs. Today's child has nothing required of them.

Cris Rowan explains how to combat this problem in today's society.

> "Whether the child's in a classroom at school or at home, the teacher and the parent create specific jobs that child does every single day. If the child doesn't do the job, then it is sorely missed. For a two-year-old, it might be that they have to take the spoons out of the dishwasher and put them in the spoon drawer. If they forget, the spoons will still in the dishwasher. This can become an issue of family importance! 'The spoons are gone, where are they? What should we do?' Obviously, this doesn't rise to the level of crisis, but it does give the child a sense that their role is important and the family is counting on them. We are meant to grow up as part of a pack and we work together as a pack. Each member of the pack has to feel important in their role."

If you think you are being kind to your child by not requiring them to do their job because they have homework or another responsibility, think again. Their self-perceived importance in the family is crucial for their development.

9. Schedule a Balance
Balance is making room for the big rocks in your child's life first. These "big rocks" are the critical factors discussed earlier:

- Touch
- Connection
- Movement
- Nature

Work to schedule and create a balance between technology use and activities involving touch, connection, movement, and nature. Instead of removing or restricting technology, focus on beefing up the four critical factors. Are children getting enough movement, touch, connection, and nature each day? If technology continues to be a problem, increase these important factors. It is more powerful and easier to institute changes, if you are trying to do something positive, rather than being perceived as only taking things away. Emphasize the positive, fun activities that can be added to your child's life and the desire to use technology will decrease, simply because there are a limited number of hours in a day.

Cris Rowan explains the balance of technology.

> "Think of technology as energy going into the body, and into the brain. Parents must balance that with energy out. Energy out means movement, touch, connection, nature. For each hour of technology, you may need to do an hour or two of a non-tech activity. A child might read to a sister, set the table, or mow the lawn. It can be chore-based or it can be freedom-based, it can't be technology based. If they don't have ideas on what they can do, brainstorm ideas, or even create a long list you can post on the fridge."

Cris' Counsel

"Follow the concept of an hour of 'energy in' (technology use) equals an hour of 'energy out' (movement, touch and connection). Make up a weekly schedule with designated time for technology, along with time for movement, touch, and connection. When beginning to unplug, alternate between familiar and new activities."

10. Create Community

Families can encourage a link between corporations and communities, to create big picture solutions to the global problem of excessive technology. Parks should develop fun activities, to be fun places to go for children, providing alternatives to being plugged in. Cris Rowan's company, Zone'in Programs Inc., suggests that all corporations involved in technology production donate a percentage of their profits toward building healthy communities. These funds might be spent on free recreation passes for children, building safe parks, and school camping trips, to help children stay unplugged. Cris says:

> "These activities are sorely lacking in our communities, especially for children over about the age of six. We need to look at our playgrounds and get more challenging things for our kids. Some parents resist going to the park because there is nothing for them to do. Funds can be used to create adult-based equipment in parks. Then parents have something to do while they watch their kids and talk to their neighbors. I think, as citizens we need to shine a light on the technology companies. Most of them have a citizenship component where they want to support community initiatives and donate money toward these things. So rather than buying new computers for everybody, they can start supporting playgrounds and different activities."

Challenges Unplugging Adolescents and Adults

How can parents unplug older teenagers and young adults? How can parents launch children into the world and into independence, while helping them avoid severe problems with technology?

> *Parent's Perspective*
> ♡ "I need help with setting boundaries for older teens and young adults. When are kids too old to be monitored? What do I do with my 21-year-old?"
>
> ~ Ann

Frankly, by the age of 12, you don't have a lot of influence on your child. You want to control your child's behavior, but the hard work has already been done. From birth to age 12, parents have quite a bit of influence, and you must use that time to shape and mold your child.

Cris Rowan explains:

> "You don't stop being a parent when they are 12 years old, it's just that they kind of quit listening to you, and your influence is gravely lowered. I'm still parenting my two children at the age of 20 and 33. I give them guidance, but I also realize that they're out in the real world and will make their own decisions. I'm focused on the ages of 0 to 12 in helping parents understand the absolute utter importance of the job that they have in parenting these children."

At the age of 12, your child's job is to start separating from you and begin making their own decisions, and it's difficult to have control in the later years. Parents can create guidelines with older children, providing regularly scheduled, technology-free family time. Cris explains how this worked in her family.

> "One hour a day was tech-free around mealtime. From dinner prep and eating, to clean-up, all technology was put somewhere else. We never ate in front of the TV. One day a week was technology free. Saturday, it was sports, or family activities, such as hiking or swimming. One week a year was technology-free. I took my kids kayaking for a week every summer, and it was something that we did together as a family. And then one week a year was the family holiday. To do that tech-free allows you to reset your relationship with your children, with your partner, and as a family, and build the family fabric, the values that make you a family. You do these regular daily, weekly, and yearly activities because that is what your family does. Kids love that kind of thing. They want to be a member, a part of your pack, of your team. So those things are just important to try too, in the exploration of alternative activities."

CHAPTER 11

Helping Children with Digital Addiction

Some children are at risk of digital addiction because of excessive technology use. Does your teen have an addiction to gaming, social media, or the internet? For help making this determination, this chapter provides some tough love for parents. You will find four different independent assessments to determine if your child has an internet or digital addiction. One simple checklist might be easy to ignore. However, if you take four different assessment tools and all four point to a serious issue, then you are more likely to pay attention. These four tools should help you break through any denial, so that you can recognize serious difficulty, and begin to address it head-on.

> ### Todd's Take
> "How many stories do we have to hear until we realize that this is really bad stuff? It doesn't occur just in the dark corners of society. It is everywhere. Parents who have guarded their children in their own homes may have them exposed to bad content in other homes. Careful parents have had their kids get up in the middle of the night to sneak online. Never assume that it's safe online, because it's not safe."

Tools for Identifying Digital Addiction

There are many words that experts use to describe this kind of addiction: digital addiction, internet addiction, computer addiction, and technology addiction in general. The addiction may be named for the specific behavior, such as gaming addiction, or online gambling addiction. Whatever you call it, these addictions must be identified before you can find appropriate resources to combat them.

Cris Rowan has been instrumental in understanding technology boundaries. This is her assessment tool for technology addiction. Three or more "yes" answers indicates a likely addiction issue.

Cris Rowan's Technology Addiction Questionnaire For All Ages[78]

1. Tolerance: "I use the same amount of technology as I used to, but it's not as much fun anymore."
2. Withdrawal: "I can't imagine going without technology."
3. Unintended Use: "I often use technology for longer than I intended."
4. Persistent Desire: "I've tried to stop using technology, but I can't."
5. Time Spent: "Technology use takes up almost all my play time."
6. Displacement of Other Activities: "I sometimes use technology when I should be spending time with my family or friends, doing my homework, or going to bed."
7. Continued Use: "I keep using technology, even though I know it isn't good for me."

Cris' Counsel

"Once the medical system starts recognizing technology addiction as an addiction, then I'm sure that there will be a

Technologic: How to Set Logical Technology Boundaries and Stop the Zombie Apocalypse

much more comprehensive addiction scale. But at this point, I often say to parents, if you can take it away and they don't complain, obviously there isn't an issue. But if you see all kinds of meltdowns and stomach aches, and can't sleep and all that, then you've got a dependence or an addiction problem."

The first and largest technology addiction recovery program in the United States offers another assessment checklist. In this assessment, three to four "yes" responses suggest abuse; five or more "yes" answers suggest addiction.

ReSTART Computer/Addiction Assessment[79]

1. Increasing amounts of time spent on computer and internet activities
2. Failed attempts to control behavior
3. Heightened sense of euphoria while involved in computer and internet activities
4. Craving more time on the computer and internet
5. Neglecting friends and family
6. Feeling restless when not engaged in the activity
7. Being dishonest with others
8. Computer use interfering with job/school performance
9. Feeling guilty, ashamed, anxious, or depressed as a result of behavior
10. Changes in sleep patterns
11. Physical changes such as weight gain or loss, backaches, headaches, carpal tunnel syndrome
12. Withdrawing from other pleasurable activities
    For further assessment tools from this resource, please see www.netaddictionrecovery.com.

Dr. Mark Griffiths is a professor in the United Kingdom, studying behavioral addictions at Nottingham Trent University in the School of Social Sciences. Dr. Mark Griffiths says internet addiction has six key criteria.

Dr. Mark Griffiths' Six Key Criteria of Internet Addiction[80]

1. Salience. The internet becomes the most important activity in the person's life, affecting feelings, behaviors, and thoughts.
2. Mood modification. The person receives an emotional "buzz" from using the internet.
3. Tolerance. The person becomes acclimatized, requiring increasing amounts of internet time to get that "buzz."
4. Withdrawal symptoms. Abruptly ceasing internet activity can cause the person emotional or physical distress.
5. Conflict. The person may be so pre-occupied with engaging in internet activities that it creates conflict with others, with work or hobbies, or inner conflicting feelings.
6. Relapse. The addict tends to fall back into the same behavior easily, even after years of abstinence or control.

The Center for Internet Addiction was founded by Dr. Kimberly Young in 1995 and provides treatment for internet addiction. Their website, NetAddiction.com, states that meeting five of the eight criteria of the Internet Addiction Diagnostic Questionnaire, below, indicates addiction.

Center for Internet Addiction Signs of Internet Addiction[81]

1. Do you feel preoccupied with the internet (think about previous online activity or anticipate next online session)?

TechnoLogic: How to Set Logical Technology Boundaries and Stop the Zombie Apocalypse

2. Do you feel the need to use the internet with increasing amounts of time in order to achieve satisfaction?
3. Have you repeatedly made unsuccessful efforts to control, cut back, or stop internet use?
4. Do you feel restless, moody, depressed, or irritable when attempting to cut down or stop internet use?
5. Do you stay online longer than originally intended?
6. Have you jeopardized or risked the loss of significant relationship, job, educational, or career opportunity because of the internet?
7. Have you lied to family members, therapist, or others to conceal the extent of involvement with the internet?
8. Do you use the internet as a way of escaping from problems or of relieving a dysphoric mood (e.g. feelings of helplessness, guilt, anxiety, depression)?

Dealing with Addiction

Cris Rowan suggests you work together with your child, and develop a personal technology reduction plan; your child signs their name and states how much they currently use technology and their goal of how many hours per day of technology they hope to stick to in future. It should also include a list of activities you can substitute for technology.

Personal Technology Reduction Plan

I, _____ plan to reduce the amount of technology use from my current _____ hours per day down to _____ hours per day.

Instead of using technology, I plan to do the following activities (circle or add new ones): biking, climbing trees, playing sports, baking, sewing, playing cards and/or board games, playing outdoor games with friends, call a friend, do volunteer work, visit elderly people, play with my bro/

sis, garden, do chores for my family, build something, take something apart, or ... (list other ideas).

Her plan continues with creating a technology schedule. Removing technology will create a gap in your child's day, like a hole in their life. It is important to replace technology with something else, so they can feel more fulfilled. It may help to create a technology schedule that includes not only what specific TV program or technology is being used along with the time, but also recommending a complimentary activity for each as well. Pick a favorite technology activity, perhaps a favorite TV show, video game, or internet activity. Schedule one hour per day, listing the specific activity and time when the activity will be done. It may help to schedule at least one hour each day for a favorite non-tech hobby or activity to do as well. Once completed, post the schedule on the fridge as a reminder for the whole family, so they know what the boundaries are within the family.

Todd's Take

"Most parents don't use technology just to pacify our children anymore, but do it to fill up all their available time. I think that's why everyone will pull out their devices at all times of the day, because they think they're not doing something important. We were in Disney World one time. My oldest was behind me on his phone while we were in line. I said, 'Hey would you get off of that?' And he said, 'What do you want me to do, just look at your back?' I said, 'Yes, that's exactly what I want you to do.' These devices are things we use just to fill up all our time."

Technologic: How to Set Logical Technology Boundaries and Stop the Zombie Apocalypse

Helping A Child Or Teen With An Internet Addiction

By far, the best way to deal with technology is to create boundaries for younger children. By the time kids are grown adults living outside the home, you have no say at all in their behavior. However, teenagers are often the biggest concern for parents. Dr. Hilarie Cash of ReSTART Net Addiction Recovery suggests specific ways to guide teenagers toward recovery.

Encourage other interests and social activities[82]

Seek out new activities for your child. Get them away from the computer screen when possible. Introduce them to new hobbies and other activities; have them join sports teams, Boy Scouts, extra-curricular activities, and clubs.

Monitor computer use and set clear limits

Set clear boundaries on digital devices with clear consequences. Use parental controls over technology so you are aware of what they can access. Keep all technology in a central area of the home where you can observe what your child is doing online. As the parent, be sure to follow the same rules yourself, because children learn by example.

Use apps to limit your child's smartphone use

Use the parental control settings on your smartphones and digital devices. There are apps to help you limit your child's smartphone use. They can monitor the phone and limit data usage, and restrict texts and web browsing. Your cell phone provider probably offers parental control. There are also apps that prevent texting and email while your teen is driving.

Talk to your child about underlying issues

Why is technology becoming a problem for your child? What issue is your child having? If there has been a change in their life recently or they're having trouble in school, it could be the

153

root of the problem. Have a frank discussion with your child. Recognize that underlying events may be a cause of addiction. Build on your child's coping skills and strengthen their support network.

Get help
Sometimes the problem is bigger than your family can handle on your own. Don't be afraid to seek help. This can be in the form of counseling, or even simple chats between your child and another adult they trust. Sometimes teens resist what their parents tell them and are more likely to listen to someone outside the family. Take it to the next step when you need more help; you can't deal with a full-blown addiction alone in your home. Tackling it on your own doesn't work for drug or alcohol addiction, and won't work for digital addiction, either.

A Digital Diet
If you want to cut back on your child's or your own internet usage, Dr. Hilarie Cash believes that a technology diet is the best start. Perhaps you and your child can go on a technology diet together. Take it one step at a time instead of cutting it out cold turkey. Give yourself one whole day of complete abstinence from everything digital; start with a one-day fast each week. This will help your receptors and dopamine levels get back in balance. Limit personal computer/device time to no more than two or three hours each day, not including use for work or school.

This tech diet will probably allow you to avoid heavy addiction. After this detox, many symptoms of depression and anxiety will clear up. Even adults experiencing attention deficit disorder traits can improve on this tech diet.

Technologic: How to Set Logical Technology Boundaries and Stop the Zombie Apocalypse

Todd's Take

"Moms and dads, don't grow weary. I know it's hard but your kids are counting on you. Just wade through it, ask forgiveness, but don't give up."

According to Cash, diagnosing patients can be complicated. With all of these problems occurring together (obsessive compulsive disorder, problems that look like autism spectrum disorder, and ADHD) they blend, making it difficult to diagnose people. Which symptoms are from internet addiction and which are unrelated? Intense gaming and internet use from an early age can result in falling behind on basic social cues, so Asperger's traits may appear.

Cash shares additional tips to help individuals regain balance.

Tips for dealing with Internet Addiction[83]

- Ask yourself, "What am I missing out on when I spend so much time on the internet?" Write down these activities and decrease your internet time to pursue some of them.
- Set reasonable internet use goals and stick to them. Take frequent breaks, at least five minutes each hour, and do some other activity.
- Alter your routine to break your usage patterns. If you spend evenings on the internet, start limiting your use to mornings.
- Seek out friends and acquaintances who "couldn't care less" about the internet. Take time to appreciate the fact that not all life is online.
- Stay connected to the offline world. Visit newsstands, book and music stores, and participate in entertainment such

as museums, music, and live theater. Novels and poetry readings are hard to experience online.
- Treat the internet as a tool. Stay focused on the fact that the internet is a means to an end. Plan your strategy—whether you're looking for information or entertainment—with the end in mind, you'll save valuable time.

Many people with digital addiction need to see a counselor. Some people have severe digital addiction, which requires in-patient treatment. An article in CNN tells the story of an accomplished writer and college professor who was laid off by a prestigious university as a result of his internet addiction. This college professor played an online game for 80 hours a week or more. He says, "I got so far into it, I couldn't realize how I got there." The professor compares his addiction to alcoholism, "A beer a day becomes a case a day. You can't stop no matter how much you want to. The real problem is that most people laugh at you and don't consider it a serious thing."[84]

President Gerald Ford's wife, Betty, was an alcoholic. When Betty Ford first admitted she was an alcoholic, people didn't believe it was a real problem. Alcoholism was seen as mostly a matter of will power than a disease. Eventually, she opened an addiction treatment center that bears her name, the Betty Ford Center. It's as important today that you speak openly about technology addiction and don't take it lightly. The professor lost not only his job, but many of his friends, and almost lost his wife as well. You can read the professor's own story about his experiences in the book, *Unplugged: My Journey into the World of Video Game Addiction*.[85]

Digital Addiction: First Person Account from a Parent's Perspective
This is a true story from a parent's point of view. It clearly conveys the seriousness of this issue, will help open your eyes, and challenge you to take action.

Technologic: How to Set Logical Technology Boundaries and Stop the Zombie Apocalypse

The Curse of Internet Addiction
A personal story of family tragedy

My husband and I dropped off our precious son at the rehab center, and went straight to a counselor's office. After an hour in tears, we next went to our first Al Anon meeting. After decades of a happy, wholesome life, our world had fallen apart completely. Our only thread to sanity was a support group for families suffering from the addictions of their loved ones. Parents and children bemoaned their loved ones' addictions to drugs and alcohol, and our beloved child was experiencing the same thing, but to the computer of all things. We were completely shocked to find ourselves in that place, feeling those feelings, and needing their support.

My son was over 21 when we recognized his digital addiction. He had graduated college and was living independently in another city for over a year when we began receiving calls each day regarding his unpaid bills. Unable to reach him for days, in desperation we drove to his home. We found him living in squalor, noticeably losing weight, and looking pale, anxious, and depressed. His speech was confused, he struggled with word choice, and he was unable to think clearly. He seemed like a completely different person than only one year prior. Over lunch, he kept his eyes covered, and repeated the phrase, "I need to think." He denied drug or alcohol use, but said he was struggling with insomnia and constant headaches. We were intensely concerned for his well-being, worried about schizophrenia or major depression. It was easy to see that he could not survive living alone.

He was thankful that we picked him up and brought him home. We immediately began seeking help from our family doctor and a psychologist because we had absolutely no clue what was happening to him.

Parent's Perspective

♡ "Our son looked like he had schizophrenia or major depression. We didn't realize it was actually digital addiction."

Once he was home, we started to notice the real problem. He was using technology for 18 hours or more each day, mostly reading fan fiction. He rarely slept, and kept his eyes glued to the computer at all times.

Our rules at home were simple: no technology in the bathroom or bedroom. While he agreed the rules were important and seemed to want to comply, he seemed unable to change his own behavior. When we found him asleep in bed with the computer on his chest, we began to keep his computer near us at night. He began to use our computer at night and lied about it, pretending it occurred while sleepwalking. Our records showed that he would spend the entire night on our computer, from 10:00 pm until we got up in the morning.

Our son had completely transformed. He had graduated Magna Cum Laude from college, but he no longer seemed smart at all. He had near perfect SAT scores, but now struggled with simple word choice, was unable to do a crossword puzzle, and had trouble understanding basic vocabulary. Our son had been outgoing, extroverted, and a social butterfly. Now he had no interests, activities, or friends, and stayed home all day. A swimmer and avid soccer player in high school, he became completely sedentary. He never went outside, never exercised, and lacked the strength and problem solving to simply open a jar of spaghetti sauce. Once a classical pianist who performed at church, he lost his ability to play the piano. His excessive reading allowed him to earn college credits at age 14, but

Technologic: How to Set Logical Technology Boundaries and Stop the Zombie Apocalypse

he had stopped reading books because they were deemed boring. His photographic memory now failed him; he constantly asked people to repeat what was said. Once close to his dad, he lashed out at his father frequently.

When he saw my husband crying, he finally began to truly listen as we explained in great detail the changes we saw in him. He agreed to get help. We sought family counseling, and learned about digital addiction for the first time. Intensive addiction counseling failed when his lying and sneaking made the program impossible. Our counselor recommended a residential treatment program.

Recognizing that this could jeopardize his financial and career plans, our son opted to give up the technology "cold turkey" and attend a 12-step recovery program. We worked together to fill our days with non-tech activities. During the first day, while baking cookies, he couldn't tell the difference between granulated sugar and powdered sugar, and even tried to crack eggs onto a plate instead of into a bowl. Within days of being media-free, we saw dramatic improvement. He became coherent, pleasant, and once again knew the day, date, and time. His vocabulary improved gradually, he began sounding "smart" again, and returned to his normal warm and loving behavior towards his father. Within a week, he could discuss his favorite political topics intelligently again, needed word-finding help only for advanced words, and was making sense most of the time in conversation. His relationship with his father was much improved.

Soon, he was able to get up in the morning, shower and shave, help with the housework, and started calling friends again. It appeared he would be able to live independently again. After several weeks of improvement, my husband and I left for a long-planned vacation, leaving our son at home with his brother. He noticed a change almost immediately, and when we returned, we could see that he had become more withdrawn. He complained again of boredom and was spending most of the day on the computer at the library. His lying began again and he became non-compliant with his counselor and 12-step program. Independent, "cold turkey" withdrawal was no longer working.

We again discussed the possibility of residential treatment, but my son was determined to manage his technology use on his own instead, while continuing therapy with a psychologist. The crisis came within a few weeks. The psychologist concluded that our son was not being truthful in sessions, but was pretending to play along so he could be deemed healthy. The psychologist explained that it is common for highly gifted and capable addicts to try to hide their addiction. He was no longer able to help our son.

We tried desperately to develop a course of action. One afternoon, my husband stumbled upon our son at the library, eyes glued to a computer screen. His transfixed, blank stare was terrifying. He didn't notice my husband six inches away, looking over his shoulder. When my husband spoke, my son was at first disoriented but then almost immediately defiant. My husband left the library in tears, knowing his son was a prisoner to something that neither of us understood. When he returned from the library that evening, our son seemed broken and said he was willing to enter residential treatment. Together, we filled out the forms and he voluntarily entered the program. The cost of treatment for six weeks was excessive, and not covered by insurance.

My husband and I began attending Al-Anon, hoping we could learn how to cope with our beloved, addicted son. He left the six-week residential treatment program seemingly healthy, with a good plan of action for his future and in the best physical shape of his life. The Asperger's symptoms that had been so pronounced when he entered the program had subsided. Tragically, the gains did not last. Although he shares little about his life, we look at the evidence and are certain he is still deeply enslaved by his addiction.

He had experienced a normal childhood within a close and loving family. During his childhood and high school years, he'd used technology only within moderation. Limited screen time had given him a wide range of activities and interests. During counseling, we came to recognize a change occurring during his college years. Reflecting back on college, we had watched our son's steady decline but didn't understand the source of his problem. As a college senior with a 3.9 GPA, he put aside his dreams of law school and started struggling academically for the first time in his life, earning his first C ever. At the time he was supposed to graduate from college, we later discovered six months' worth of classes were incomplete. It took him another year to complete those few classes and earn his degree. He found a great job after graduation but was fired after three months for unauthorized technology use on the job. He was offered another high-paying job, but didn't respond to the offer in time to accept the job.

Since he was no longer in college or employed, spending his time on the couch in pajamas all day, we had told him to move out of our home. We had no idea what was causing his behavior. He began to live with people he did not know, paying rent for a bed he could sleep on, living out of boxes in a room he shared with another fellow. This was how we found him the day we brought our adult son back home.

What is digital addiction like? When our son overuses the internet, he appears to be mentally ill, becoming withdrawn, angry, and sullen. His symptoms mimic Asperger's Syndrome. He will not eat, sleep, wash, or perform normal daily activities. He has trouble thinking clearly, struggles with word choice, lies excessively, and is untrustworthy. He will not socialize, mumbles frequently, and seems incapable of holding a conversation. He is lost and stuck, unable to act as an adult. In contrast, when he is not overindulging in internet use, he is pleasant, cheerful, charming, good-natured, and brilliant. He can be the smartest person we know, with an extensive vocabulary, excellent grasp of almost every subject, and an easy laugh.

We constantly pray for him to become mentally and physically healthy, and to eventually have a home and a job, but he is no longer a child. We are constantly challenged as we try to balance our love and care for him with our firm commitment to avoid enabling behavior. We want him to become a successful, thriving adult, but we recognize it is out of our control; only he can take the necessary steps, now that he is an adult. We see and feel the waste of his amazing, God-given gifts. We know that God isn't through with our son but have no idea when he will be able to throw off the shackles of his addiction, so he can begin to live his life again.

~ Anonymous Mom

CONCLUSION

Doing Everything Right is No Guarantee

When reading stories of families dealing with their kids' serious addiction issues, the natural tendency is to think there must have been something, some defect in their family life, that resulted in the addiction. It is part of human desire to find a reasonable cause for every result.

Sometimes life isn't that easy or convenient. The anonymous mom who shared her story in the previous chapter wrote the following summary of their family and their children's upbringing. As you will see, there was no alcoholism, abuse, anger, divorce, or any other apparent dysfunction. Sometimes bad things happen. Sometimes you can do everything right and still have it turn out wrong. It's the way life is sometimes. Read this postscript, and understand the seriousness of your responsibilities as a parent.

> As a fallible human, I know that I'm not perfect, and my family isn't perfect. But when I look back through the years, I can't see anything that might have caused or enabled internet addiction in our family. We don't know why it happened, or what made it so severe. When we first placed our child into a treatment facility, I was stunned. I truly believe I did everything right, as much as possible, as an imperfect person living in an imperfect world.

Our family has always been solid.
My husband and I have been married for over 30 years. We have always had a close, loving relationship. In our extended family, there has not been a single divorce or separation. We love our family and love our God. Our children were best friends, with a warm relationship. My husband gave up career advancement and travel to devote his time to what he considered his higher calling - fathering our children. He changed his work schedule to be with the family as many hours as possible during the day. We were involved in sports, coaching and often attending games and practices four to six days a week. Our children had weekly activities in art and music lessons, and we attended our kids' events even when they didn't interest us as parents. As a family, we all attended church, and my kids went to the youth group. We homeschooled for academic reasons, but our children had many friends and teammates they played with. They were both social children.

Our vacations were camping, hiking, biking, and touring our city. We traveled to exciting places sometimes, creating great family memories of the Caribbean, Mount Rushmore, Washington DC and fun theme parks. When the kids were younger, our home was filled with roughhousing, Nerf wars, and water fights. When our children were older, our roughhousing and competitiveness took place at the community pool. We had breakfast, lunch, and dinner together most days, and on weekends we spent time with extended family.

Our technology was always limited.
All technology was clearly in view and easily seen by parents. There was no technology of any kind in our bedrooms; it was limited only to family areas, during the daytime. Our time limits were firm, with half an hour each day during elementary school, expanding to one hour a day during middle school

until the transition to adulthood. We raised our kids in the dial-up internet age, so there was nothing much of interest online, except for email, which our children did not have. We homeschooled, but used non-tech curriculum, with rare exceptions. They worked with the computer, but only for learning to type, writing, or research, closely monitored by a parent. They received their own basic cell phone when they entered the workforce, and were expected to stay in touch while at work.

Our values and convictions were clear.
As a Christian family, we worked together, prayed together, cleaned the house and mowed the yard together. We all worked hard. My husband and I prayed for our children and their futures daily. My children each had a job when they turned 14-years-old. My son even wrote a novel about the value of hard work. We raised our children to be independent, carefully explaining that we would support an adult child only while they attended college full time, or for the first year of full time employment. They paid for their own cars, when they needed one. They developed unique and passionate interests that would lead to quality college degrees and great opportunities for employment.

Our expectations were normal.
Knowing we live in an imperfect world, we had no expectations of perfect children. We supervised, researched, and were careful in our choices. We didn't expect them to know what to do. We taught them, then showed them, then allowed them to practice skills, before living on their own. They attended a small Christian university near our home, to spread their wings while being near a support system. Our children truly did thrive as they became adults, and experienced huge successes.

And then came the change.
We noticed huge problems toward the end of college. Our job had been done for years, and our children were independent except for some help with living expenses prior to graduation. Everything was going great. That was when we realized our now-adult son had gradually developed an internet addiction. We had done everything we could do. We raised them with technology boundaries. We sent them into the world with the skills they needed, and still had a "crash and burn" scenario.

I wish ...
I wish we had known about digital addiction before my children went to college. I talked to them about alcohol, drugs, sex, and eating disorders. I didn't know about digital addiction, or I would have included that in our discussions. We didn't know what was happening until it was too late. My son didn't realize what was happening to himself, either. After all, his friends all consumed digital technology, without seeming to have any problems. How could we have known?

Still, no amount of talking or education would necessarily have made a difference. By the time they enter college, teens are largely independent and make their own decisions. Our son one time brought home his TV from college when he recognized he was wasting too much time watching it. He seemed to have some awareness at that time of the trouble that could come from too much screen time. Digital addiction was something that snuck up on all of us. Tendencies that might now be seen only in retrospect came to full and poisonous blossom during that last year of college.

In a sense, we feel victimized by technology. While it is clear to everyone that drugs and alcohol are dangerous, there were few red flags associated with technology.

Technologic: How to Set Logical Technology Boundaries and Stop the Zombie Apocalypse

Because my son's addiction had nothing to do with the areas we had discussed with him (porn, excessive gaming, and gambling), none of us saw the danger. This proved to be the fatal factor. If a danger is not recognized quickly and dealt with, it can be overwhelming.

We know that God isn't done with our son or our family. As long as we have breath, my husband and I will love and pray for our adult sons. My husband joked the other day that God must have given us children because he knew how much we needed something to worry about. Funny, but perhaps the truth is God knows how much we need to understand our dependence on Him and stay on our knees before Him.

Please tell your children about digital addiction, and warn them about the signs and symptoms of abuse in themselves and in their friends. Hopefully you can catch it before a serious problem develops. Because even if you do everything right, it's possible for your child to develop a serious technology problem. If you learn more about it, and educate your children, you may be able to avoid the problems we continue to face with our son who is battling a serious addiction.

~ Anonymous Mom

Like many challenges in life, happy endings are not guaranteed. It's important to recognize that every family has before them battles they must fight. You need to be compassionate and understanding as you encounter these families, and educate yourself to avoid the same problems in your own home.

No less authority than Eric Schmit, the Executive Chairman of Google says, "The Internet is the first thing that humanity has built that humanity doesn't understand." When the chairman of the world's premier technology company admits people don't know what they have built, you need to take notice.

Parents, who carefully check labels to ensure the food and clothing they give to their children is safe, are blindly feeding them what is brought forward by internet marketers and self-proclaimed education experts. The truth is, the internet has exploded on society so quickly that the research of its impact has not had a chance to catch up. It is both prudent and wise, then, that you proceed with a healthy skepticism about what you allow to enter the minds of your defenseless children and easily influenced young adults. Do not allow your family to be swept along by the fashionable currents of this time. The flow is fast and the waters are deep. You may not be able to avoid the water completely, but you can certainly put on life jackets and teach your children how to navigate the swiftly flowing stream.

About the Author

Number one homeschooling author, convention speaker, and coach, Lee Binz, is The HomeScholar. Her mission is "helping parents homeschool high school." Lee and her husband, Matt, homeschooled their two boys from elementary through high school. Upon graduation, both boys received four-year, full-tuition scholarships from their first choice university. This enabled Lee to pursue her dream job, encouraging parents to homeschool their children through high school.

Lee is the author of *Setting the Records Straight: How to Craft Homeschool Transcripts and Course Descriptions for College Admission and Scholarships*, *The HomeScholar Guide to College Admission and Scholarships: Homeschool Secrets for Getting Ready, Getting In, and Getting Paid*, and *Finding the Faith to Homeschool High School: Weekly Devotions for Weary Parents*. She has also authored an extremely popular series of short, helpful books she calls, "Coffee Break Books". Lee loves speaking at homeschool conventions and her dynamic presentations leave parents feeling confident and capable.

You can find Lee online at www.TheHomeScholar.com and on Facebook. For help, please email Lee@TheHomeScholar.com.

Resources

Companion Video Series

Did you know? This book has a companion video series with handouts, audio downloads, live and recorded webinar presentations! View the series online for additional encouragement and information!

TechnoLogic: Critical Technology Boundaries for Children and Teens
www.TheHomeScholar.com/TechnoLogic.php

"Your candidness ministered to me as a mom and teacher of my children."

~ Connie

"These are topics that unfortunately are much needed topics in today's world. It takes courage to address these issues. Thank you for the balance of honesty and sensitivity with which you addressed them. Thank you for taking on these topics and doing such a great job with them!"

~ Cyndie

"I have five sons, ranging in ages from 14 - 22. Two of my sons have confessed an addiction to pornography. They were initially exposed to it by their cousin's thumb drive pictures and I have since become aware that some of the video games that they play online have been "popping up" photos as well. They continue to struggle to be free of what is in their head. I now suspect that my oldest son has, at the very least, a technology addiction as well. Thank you for opening my eyes wider."

~ Elizabeth

APPENDIX A

Critical Technology Boundaries for Children and Teens Worksheet

Name some reasons why it's important to set boundaries on technology.

_____
_____
_____
_____
_____
_____
_____
_____
_____
_____
_____
_____
_____

List ways parents can create wholesome technology boundaries.

_____
_____

Lee Binz, The HomeScholar

What ideas for technology boundaries will you implement in your home?

List the long-term consequences of excessive technology use.

Technologic: How to Set Logical Technology Boundaries and Stop the Zombie Apocalypse

List the symptoms of serious technology abuse.

Assess the risk of internet addiction within your family with these tools.

Parent-Child Internet Addiction Test:
http://netaddiction.com/parent-child-internet-addiction-test/

Internet Addiction Self-Test:
http://netaddiction.com/self-tests/

Signs & Symptoms of Computer & Internet/Gaming Addiction:
http://www.netaddictionrecovery.com/the-problem/signs-and-symptoms.html

APPENDIX B

Reference Charts from Zone'in Programs Inc.

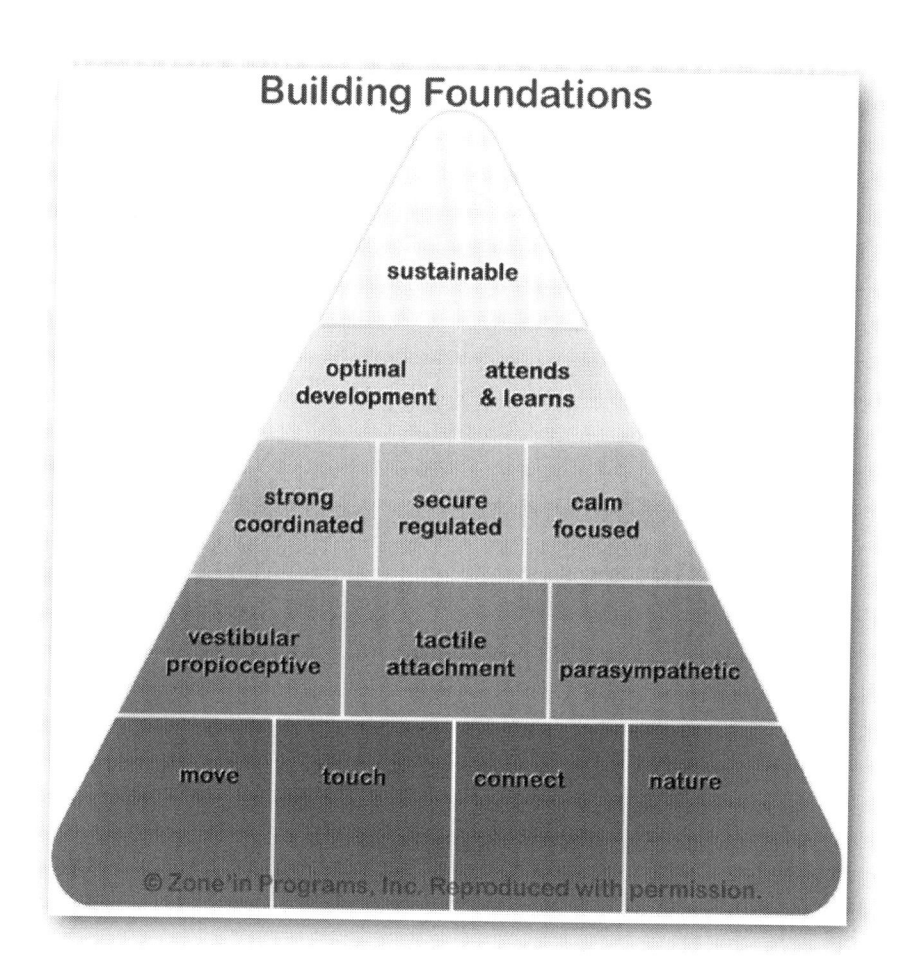

Building Foundations

- sustainable
- optimal development | attends & learns
- strong coordinated | secure regulated | calm focused
- vestibular propioceptive | tactile attachment | parasympathetic
- move | touch | connect | nature

© Zone'in Programs, Inc. Reproduced with permission.

Lee Binz, The HomeScholar

Virtual Futures

TV	cellphone	internet
sedentary	isolated	neglected	overstumulated

developmental delay / obesity	mental illnes / detached	ADHD / autism

| • diabetes
• stroke
• ♥ attack | • addicted
• violent
• perverted | • compulsive
• medicated
• illiterate |

| early death | no relationship | no job |

unsustainable

© Zone'in Programs, Inc.
Reproduced with permission.

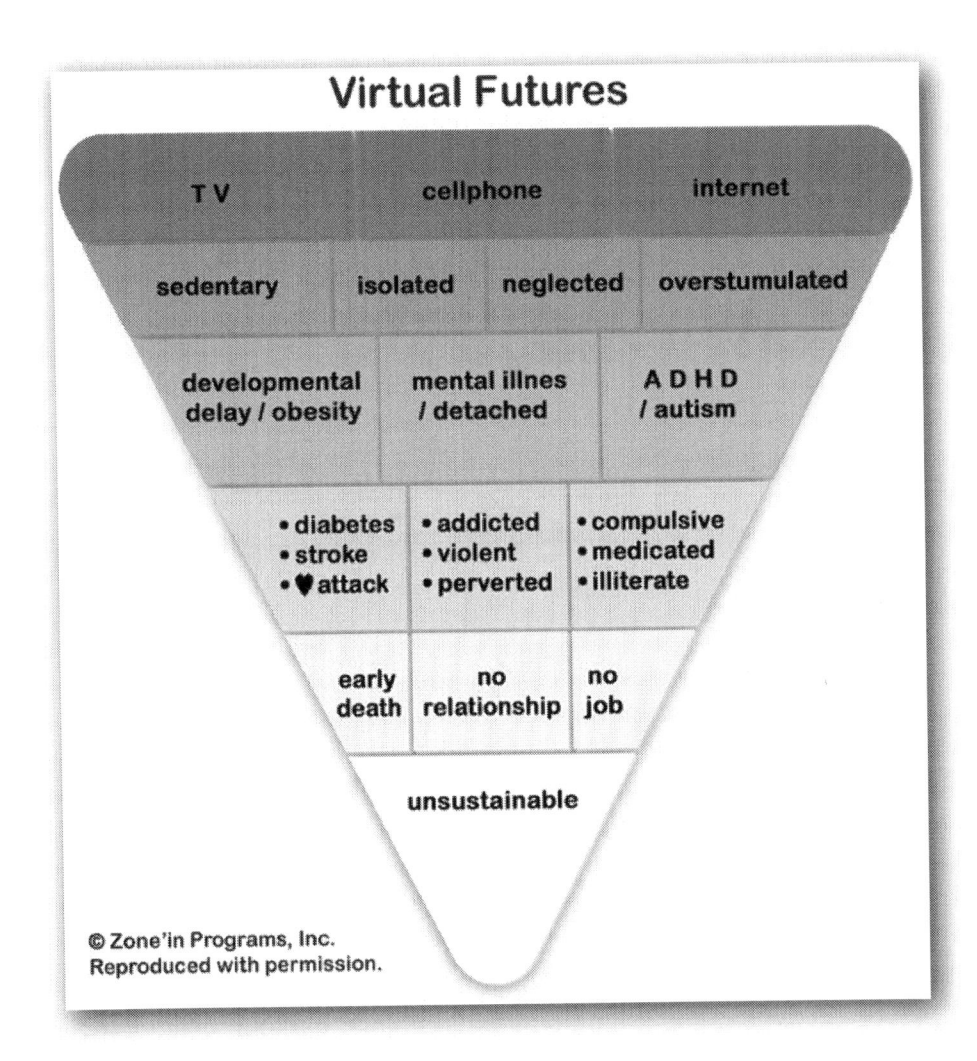

180

Technologic: How to Set Logical Technology Boundaries and Stop the Zombie Apocalypse

Technology Use Guidelines for Children and Youth

Developmental Age	How Much	Non-Violent TV	Handheld devices	Non-Violent Video Games	Violent Video games	Online Violent Video Games or Pornography
0 - 2 Years	none	never	never	never	never	never
3 - 5 Years	1 hour a day	✓	never	never	never	never
6 - 12 Years	2 hours a day	✓	never	never	never	never
13 - 18 Years	2 hours a day	✓	✓	limit to 30 minutes a day	limit to 30 minutes a day	never

Please contact Cris Rowan at info@zonein.ca for additional information. © Zone'in

APPENDIX C

Resources

Books for Parents

Wilson, Todd. *Taming the Techno-Beast, Helping You Understand and Navigate Your Child's Electronic World.* Indiana: Familyman Ministries, 2009. Print. Kindle e-book.

Wilson, Todd. *Taming the Techno-Beast, Student Workbook.* Indiana: Familyman Ministries, 2013. Print.

Cash, Hilarie, and Kim McDaniel. *Video Games & Your Kids: How Parents Stay in Control.* Pennsylvania State University: Issues Press, 2008. Print.

Rowan, Ms. Cris A. *Virtual Child: The terrifying truth about what technology is doing to children.* Sechelt, British Columbia: CreateSpace Independent Publishing Platform, 2010. Print.

Doan, Andrew P, Brooke Strickland, and Douglas Gentile. *Hooked on Games: The Lure and Cost of Video Game and Internet Addiction.* Coralville, Iowa: FEP International, 2012. Print.

Stafford, Rachel Macy. *Hands Free Life: Nine Habits for Overcoming Distraction, Living Better, and Loving More.* Zondervan, 2015. Print. Kindle e-book. Audio.

Rosen, Larry D. *iDisorder: Understanding Our Obsession with Technology and Overcoming Its Hold on Us.* St. Martin's Griffin, 2013. Print. Kindle e-book. Audio.

Dunckley, Victoria L. *Reset Your Child's Brain: A Four-Week Plan to End Meltdowns, Raise Grades, and Boost Social Skills by Reversing the Effects of Electronic Screen Time.* New World Library, 2015. Print. Kindle e-book.Steyer, James P. Talking Back to Facebook: The Common Sense Guide to Raising Kids in the Digital Age. Scribner, 2012. Print. Kindle e-book.

Sax, Leonard. *Boys Adrift: The Five Factors Driving the Growing Epidemic of Unmotivated Boys and Underachieving Young Men.* New York: Basic Books, 2009. Print. Kindle e-book.

Carnes, Patrick J., David L. Delmonico, Elizabeth Griffin, and Joseph M. Moriarity *In the Shadows of the Net: Breaking Free of Compulsive Online Sexual Behavior.* Hazelden, 2007. Print. Kindle e-book.

Young, Kimberly S. and Cristiano Nabuco de Abreu. *Internet Addiction: A Handbook and Guide to Evaluation and Treatment.* Wiley, 2010. Print. Kindle e-book.

Young, Kimberly S. *Tangled in the Web: Understanding Cybersex from Fantasy to Addiction.* Authorhouse, 2001. Print.

Steiner-Adair, Catherine. *The Big Disconnect: Protecting Childhood and Family Relationships in the Digital Age.* Harper, 20013. Print. Kindle e-book.

Mander, Jerry. *Four Arguments for the Elimination of Television.* Avon, 2013. Print. Kindle e-book.

Postman, Neil. *Technopoly: The Surrender of Culture to Technology.* Vintage, 2011. Print. Kindle e-book.

Healy, Jane M. *Endangered Minds: Why Children Don't Think – and What We Can Do About It.* Simon & Schuster, 1999. Print. Kindle e-book.

Healy, Jane M. *Failure to Connect: How Computers Affect Our Children's Minds - For Better and Worse.* Simon & Schuster, 1999. Print. Kindle e-book.

Thompson, Damian. *The Fix: How Addiction is Taking Over Your World.* Collins, 2012. Print.

Louv, Richard. *Last Child in the Woods: Saving Our Children from Nature-Deficit Disorder.* Algonquin Books, 2008. Print. Kindle e-book.

Gurian, Michael and Kathy Stevens. *The Minds of Boys: Saving Our Sons from Falling Behind in School and Life.* Jossey-Bass, 2009. Print. Kindle e-book.

Berk, Laura E. *Awakening Children's Minds: How Parents and Teachers Can Make a Difference.* Oxford University Press, 2004. Print.

Maté, Gabor. *Scattered Minds: A New Look at the Origin and Healing of Attention Deficit Disorder.* Vintage Canada, 2011. Print. Kindle e-book.

Books for Kids

Jenson, Kristen A. *Good Pictures Bad Pictures: Porn-Proofing Today's Young Kids.* Glen Cove Press, 2014. Print. Kindle e-book.

Websites
The HomeScholar: www.thehomescholar.com

Familyman Ministries: http://familymanweb.com

reSTART Internet Addiction Recovery Program: www.netaddictionrecovery.com

Common Sense Media: www.commonsensemedia.org

Zone'in – programs, workshops, consultations, training: www.zonein.ca

Unplugged Challenge – community programs to unplug: www.unpluggedchallenge.com

Real Battle Ministries – video game addiction: www.realbattle.org

SOS Parents – brain changes from video games: www.sosparents.org

EU Kids Online – collated research: www.lse.ac.ak

TechAddiction – online help network: www.techaddiction.ca

Hands Free Mama - support for reducing parental use of technology: www.handsfreemama.com

Stop Porn Culture: www.stoppornculture.org

On Line Gamers Anonymous: www.olganon.org

Quibly – for parents who want to balance technology with life: www.quibly

Wowaholics – World of Warcraft addicts: www.wowaholics.org/home

TVO Parents – parent help: www.tvoparents.tvo.org/

Children Now – impact of media on children: www.childrennow.org

Center on Media and Child Health – research and tips: www.cmch.tv

National Institute on Media and the Family: www.mediafamily.org

Young Media Australia – for youth: www.youngmedia.org

Family Media Guide: www.familymediaguide.com

Campaign for a Commercial Free Childhood: www.commericalexploitation.org

Dr. Peter Breggin – info on child psychotropic medication mania: www.breggin.com

Mothers of Bad Boys – your boys aren't bad: www.mothersofbadboys.com

Parents for Safe Technology – on dangers of WiFi radiation: www.parentsforsafetechnology.org

Parental Control Software/Internet Filters

<u>Recommended by Kim McDaniel:</u>
Net Nanny: www.netnanny.com

McAfee Family Protection: http://home.mcafee.com/store/family-protection

Others available:
Covenant Eyes: www.covenanteyes.com

Web Watcher Now: www.webwatchernow.com

Cyber Patrol: www.cyberpatrol.com

Safe Eyes: www.internetsafety.com

Mobicip: www.mobicip.com

ScreenRetriever: www.screenretriever.com

K9 Web Protection: www1.k9webprotection.com

North American Technology Addiction Treatment Centers

United States
Seattle, Washington - ReSTART Internet Addiction and Recovery: www.netaddictionrecovery.com

Hartford, Connecticut - Center for Internet and Technology Addiction: www.virtual-addiction.com

Pittsburgh, Pennsylvania - Bradford Regional Medical Center: www.netaddiction.com

Canada
New Westminster, British Columbia – Last Door: www.lastdoor.org

Other
National Suicide Prevention Lifeline: In the U.S. call 1-800-273-8255

APPENDIX D

Works Cited

1. News Service. "ISU's Gentile authors study finding nearly 1 in 10 youth gamers addicted to video games." Iowa State University. n.pag. Web. 20 Apr. 2009.

2. Ryall, Julian. "Surge in Digital Dementia." The Telegraph. n. pag. Web. 24 Jun. 2013.

3. Ward, Victoria. "Toddlers becoming addicted to iPads." The Telegraph. n. pag. Web. 21 Apr. 2013.

4. Ablow, Dr. Keith. "Technology problems may be the tobacco industry of our times." Fox News. n. pag. Web. 19 Aug. 2013.

5. Flux, Elizabeth. "Google Maps Has Been Tracking Your Every Move, And There's A Website To Prove It." Junkee. n. pag. Web. 15 Aug. 2014.

6. O'Donnell, Andy. "5 Things You Should Never Post on Facebook." About.com: About Tech. n. pag. Web. n.d.

7. Associated Press. "Chicago-Area Students Face Child Porn Charges." CBS St. Louis. n. pag. Web. 2 May 2014.

8. US Dept of Health & Human Services. "What is Cyberbullying?" stopbullying.gov. n.p. n.d. Web. 2014.

9. Perry, L. David. "The Impact of Technology on Children." American College of Pediatricians. n. pag. Web. Oct. 2015.

10. Moore, Abby. "The day my kid found hardcore porn on his iPhone." LifeSiteNews. n. pag. Web. 17 Jul. 2014.

11. O'Leary, Amy. "So How Do We Talk About This? When Children See Internet Pornography." The New York Times: Home & Garden. n. pag. Web. 9 May 2012.

12. Post Staff Report. "Email Addiction." New York Post. n. pag. Web. 26 Jul. 2007.

13. Hatfield, Heather. "Power Down for Better Sleep." WebMD: Sleep Disorders Health Center. n. pag. Web. n.d.

14. Jamwal, Dr. Manika. "Tired? Try these sleep tips." The Seattle Times. n. pag. Web. 21 Oct. 2014.

15. Ubaid, Muhammad. "A Texting Guy Almost Runs into a Wild Bear." YouTube. Video. 15 Apr. 2012.

16. Silva, Cristina. "Deadly Selfie: Couple Dies After Taking Selfie While Vacationing in Portugal In Latest Selfie-Related Death." International Business Times. n. pag. Web. 11 Aug. 2014.

17. "This Is How The Internet Is Rewiring Your Brain." The Huffington Post. n. pag. 30 Oct. 2013.

18. Hu, Elise. "Facebook Makes Us Sadder And Less Satisfied, Study Finds." All Tech Considered. n. pag. Web. 20 Aug. 2013.

19. Taylor, Jim. "How Technology is Changing the Way Children Think and Focus." Psychology Today. n. pag. Web. 4 Dec. 2012.

20. Grandoni, Dino. "The Disturbing New Trend In 'Grand Theft Auto' Is Virtual Rape." The Huffington Post. n. pag. Web. 12 Aug. 2014.

21. Romano, Michaela, Lisa A. Osborne, Roberto Truzoli, and Phil Reed. "Differential Psychological Impact of Internet Exposure on Internet Addicts." PLOS. n. pag. Web. 7 Feb. 2013.

22. Anderson, Pauline. "Brain Abnormalities Linked to 'Internet Addiction'" Medscape. n. pag. Web. 5 May, 2014.

23. Naish, John. "How gadgets and the internet are turning us into a nation of emotional basket cases." Daily Mail. n. pag. Web. 19 July 2012.

24. Rosen, Larry. "Face the Facts: We Are All Headed for an 'iDisorder.'" Psychology Today. n. pag. Web. 28 Mar. 2012.

25. Wong, David. "5 Creepy Ways Video Games Are Trying to Get You Addicted." Cracked. n. pag. Web. 8 Mar. 2010

26. Henn, Scott. "Kids' Video Games: Source of Fun, Pain, and Profit." KQED Inc.: Mind/Shift. n. pag. Web. 29 Oct. 2013.

27. Tropf, Lindsey. "About." Immersed Games. n. pag. n.d. Web. 2014.

28. Rowan, Cris. "10 Reasons Why Handheld Devices Should Be Banned for Children Under the Age of 12." The Huffington Post. n. pag. Web. 6 Mar. 2014.

29. Gentile, Douglas A et al. "The Effects of Prosocial Video Games on Prosocial Behaviors." Personality and Social Psychology Bulletin. Sage Journals. 25 Mar. 2009.

30. Greitemeyer, Tobias and Dirk O. Mugge. "Video Games Do Affect Social Outcomes." Personality and Social Psychology Bulletin. 40.5. (2014): 578-589. Print. Web.

31. Price-Mitchell, Marilyn. "Impact of Media: Are We Over-Stimulating Young Children?" Roots of Action. n. pag. Web. 13 Feb. 2012.

32. Tremblay, M.S. "Temporal trends in overweight and obesity in Canada," 1981-1996. National Center for Biotechnology Information. n. pag. Web. 26 Apr. 2002.

33. Flores, Philip J. *Addiction as an Attachment Disorder.* Jason Aronson Inc. 2004. Print.

34. Kuo, F.E., & Faber Taylor, A. (2004). "A potential natural treatment for Attention-Deficit/Hyperactivity Disorder: Evidence from a national study." American Journal of Public Health, 94(9): 1580-1586.

35. Wilson, Lauren. "Yes, This Is Happening: VTech Just Made a Tablet for Your 12-Month-Old." All Things Digital. n. pag. Web. 6 May 2013.

36. "How Technology is Having a Serious Impact on Your Child's Development." The Huffington Post UK. n. pag. Web. 15 Sep. 2014.

37. Graff, Amy. "Today's kids better at using smartphone than tying their shoes." San Francisco Gate. n. pag. Web. 10 Sep. 2014.

38. "Internet Gaming Disorder." DSM5.org n. pag. Web. May 2013.

39. Ablow, Dr. Keith. "Studies show Facebook may be true, significant public health threat." Fox News. n. pag. Web. 19 Aug. 2013.

40. Hill, Kashmir. "Facebook Manipulated 689,003 Users' Emotions For Science." Forbes. n. pag. Web. 28 Jun. 2014.

41. Whitbourne, Susan Krauss. "Your Smartphone May Be Making You ... Not Smart." Psychology Today. n. pag. Web. 18 Oct. 2014.

42. "'Digital dementia' on the rise as young people increasingly rely on technology instead of their brain." Daily Mail. n. pag. Web. 24 Jun. 2013.

43. Gregoire, Carolyn. "How Technology Is Warping Your Memory." The Creativity Post. n. pag. Web. 1 May 2014.

44. Romeo, Nick. "Is Google Making Students Stupid?" The Atlantic. n. pag. Web. 30 Sep. 2014.

45. Carr, Nicholas. *The Glass Cage: Automation and Us.* WW Norton, 2014. Print. Kindle e-book.

46. "Students and Video Game Addiction." Inside Higher Ed. Web. n. pag. Web. 13 Dec. 2012.

47. Lifespan. "Texting, social networking and other media use linked to poor academic performance." Science Daily. n. pag. Web. 11 Apr 2013.

48. Shirky, Clay. "Why Clay Shirky Banned Laptops, Tablets and Phones from His Classroom." PBS: MediaShift. n. pag. Web. 15 Sep. 2014.

49. Sana, Faria. "Laptop Multitasking Hinders Classroom Learning for Both Users and Nearby Peers." Science Direct: Computers & Education. n. pag. Web. March 2013.

50. Adams, Sam. "Spending too much time online 'causing mental illness in children' government health advisers warn." Mirror. n. pag. Web. 16 May 2014.

51. "Growing Up Online." PBS Frontline video. Web. 2008.

52. Hathaway, Jay. "A Call of Duty Loser Called the SWAT Team on His Opponent." Gawker. n. pag. Web. 23 Apr. 2014.

53. Wilson, Gary. "The great porn experiment." YouTube: TEDx Talks. n. pag. Web. 16 May 2012. Video.

54. Huffman, Mark. "When does cell phone dependence become addiction?" Consumer Affairs. n. pag. Web. 4 Sep. 2014.

55. Walker, Lauren. "Man is Treated in First Case of Google Glass Addiction." Newsweek. n. pag. Web. 15 Oct. 2014.

56. Cash, Hilarie. "Warning Signs and Symptoms." reSTART. n. pag. Web. 2014.

57. Shute, Nancy. "Dry, Scratchy Eyes? Staring At Screens Is Driving This Trend." Shots: Health News from NPR. n. pag. Web. 4 Sep. 2014.

58. Santos, Zeon. "Trailer For Love Child - A Documentary About Internet Addiction." Neatorama. n. pag. Web. 23 Jan. 2014.

59. Rowan, Cris. "The Impact of Technology on the Developing Child" The Huffington Post. n. pag. Web. 29 May. 2013.

60. Inbar, Michael. "Mom's hug revives baby that was pronounced dead." TODAY. n. pag. Web. 3 Sep. 2010.

61. "Americans eat out about 5 times a week." UPI. n. pag. Web. 19 Sep. 2011.

62. Kuo, F.E., & Faber Taylor, A. (2004). "A potential natural treatment for Attention-Deficit/Hyperactivity Disorder: Evidence from a national study." American Journal of Public Health, 94(9): 1580-1586.

63. Singh, Amika, Leonie Uijdewilligen, Jos W. R. Twisk, Willem van Mechelen, Mai J. M. Chinapaw. "Physical Activity and Performance at School." JAMA Pediatrics. (2012). Print.

64. Rowan, Cris. "Zone'in Fact Sheet: A research review regarding the impact of technology on child development, behavior, and academic performance." Zone'in. n. pag. Web. 13 Aug. 2015.

65. Romeo, Nick. "Is Google Making Students Stupid?" The Atlantic. n. pag. Web. 30 Sep. 2014.

66. Park, Alice. "Baby Einsteins: Not So Smart After All." Time. n. pag. Web. 6 Aug. 2007.

67. Ratey, John. *Spark*. Little, Brown and Company. 2008. Print. Kindle e-book.

68. Eldeib, Duaa. "Barrington police investigate middle school 'sexting.'" Chicago Tribune. n. pag. Web. 8 Apr. 2014.

69. Rowan, Cris. "10 Reasons Why Handheld Devices Should Be Banned for Children Under the Age of 12." The Huffington Post. n. pag. Web. 6 Mar. 2014.

70. "Privacy and Internet Safety." Common Sense Media. n. pag. Web. n.d.

71. Fields, Lisa. "6 Ways Pets Can Improve Your Health." WebMD. n. pag. Web. n.d.

72. Scott, Jane. "Comment: Parenting while distracted." SBS. n. pag. Web. 11 Aug. 2014.

73. Bilton, Nick. "Steve Jobs Was a Low-Tech Parent." New York Times. n. pag. Web. 10 Sep. 2014.

74. "Children, Adolescents, and the Media." Pediatrics. Volume 132. Issue 5. n. pag. Web. 2013.

75. Rowan, Cris. "10 steps to successfully unplug children from technology." Moving to Learn. n. pag. Web. 18 Mar. 2014.

76. Kuo, Frances E. "Green Play Settings Reduce ADHD Symptoms." University of Illinois. n. pag. Web. n.d.

77. Kuo, Frances E. and Andrea Faber Taylor. "A Potential Natural Treatment for Attention-Deficit/Hyperactivity Disorder: Evidence from a National Study." National Center for Biotechnology Information. n. pag. Web. Sep. 2004.

78. Rowan, Cris. "Technology Addiction Questionnaire." Zonein. ca. n. pag. Web. n.d.

79. "Signs & Symptoms of Internet Gaming Addiction." restart. n. pag. Web. n.d.

80. Griffiths, Mark. "A Brief Overview of Behavioral Addictions." Addiction.com. n. pag. Web. 13 Feb. 2015.

81. Young, Kimberly "Signs of Internet Addiction." NetAddiction. n. pag. Web. n.d.

82. Saisan, Joanna. Melinda Smith, Lawrence Robinson, and Jeanne Seagal. "Internet and Computer Addiction: Helping a child or teen with an Internet addiction." Helpguide.org. n. pag. Web. n.d.

83. Saisan, Joanna, Melinda Smith, Lawrence Robinson, and Jeanne Seagal. "Internet and Computer Addiction: Tips for dealing with internet addiction." Helpguide.org. n. pag. Web. n.d.

84. Tinker, Ben. "Four beds ready to treat Internet addicts." CNN. n. pag. Web. 7 Sep. 2013.

85. Van Cleave, Ryan G. *Unplugged: My Journey into the Dark World of Video Game Addiction.* HCI, 2010. Print. Kindle e-book.

Made in the USA
San Bernardino, CA
27 July 2017